A Special Gift

With Love,

Date

*A Story Collection That Touches
the Heart as Only a Hug Can Do*

hugs™

for the
HEART

COMPILED BY RHONDA HOGAN

PATSY CLAIRMONT • FLORENCE LITTAUR
AURTHUR GORDON • ZIG ZIGLAR
ALAN LOY MCGINNIS • RAVI ZACHARIAS

HOWARD BOOKS
® A DIVISION OF SIMON & SCHUSTER
New York   London   Toronto   Sydney

Our purpose at Howard Books is to:
- *Increase faith* in the hearts of growing Christians
- *Inspire holiness* in the lives of believers
- *Instill hope* in the hearts of struggling people everywhere
Because He's coming again!

Published by Howard Books, a division of Simon and Schuster, Inc.
1230 Avenue of the Americas, New York, NY 10020
www.howardpublishing.com

Hugs for the Heart © 2007 by Howard Books

Library of Congress Cataloging-in-Publication Data
Hugs for the heart / compiled by Rhonda Hogan.
p. cm.
    1. Christian life.   2. Christian life--Anecdotes.   I. Hogan, Rhonda S.
BV4515.3.H84 2007
242—dc222006021600

ISBN-10 1-4165-3582-9; ISBN 13: 978-1-4165-3582-9
ISBN-10 1-58229-668-5; ISBN-13: 978-1-58229-668-5

10 9 8 7 6 5 4 3 2 1

HOWARD colophon is a registered trademark of Simon & Schuster, Inc.
Manufactured in the United States of America

For information regarding special discounts for bulk purchases, please contact:
Simon & Schuster Special Sales at 1-800-456-6798 or
business@simonandschuster.com.

Edited by Philis Boultinghouse
Cover design by John Lucas

Scripture quotations not otherwise marked are from the *Holy Bible, New International Version*®. Copyright © 1973, 1978, 1984 by International Bible Society. Used by permission of Zondervan. All rights reserved. Scripture quotations marked KJV are taken from the *King James Version* of the Bible. Public domain. The Madeline L'Engle reference on pages 107 and 110 is from *A Wind in the Door* (New York: Farrar Straus & Giroux, 1973), 97–99.

Contents

Contents

Contents

Chapter Six
Hugs Make Music in the Heart

Chapter Seven
Hugs Create Joy in the Heart

Contents

CHAPTER EIGHT
Hugs Are Touches of the Heart

Blessed are those who see the hand of God in the haphazard, inexplicable, and seemingly senseless circumstances of life.

ERWIN W. LUTZER

CHAPTER ONE

Hugs Are Gifts from the Heart

Kindness is more than deeds.

It is an attitude, an expression,

a look, a touch. It is anything

that lifts another person.

C. NEIL STRAIT

MIDDLE MAN

Patsy Clairmont

*B*ecause of a delay in taking off, my homebound flight was late, leaving me at risk of missing my second plane. When we landed at the connecting airport, I rushed through the terminal, arriving at my gate just as they were closing the doors. Relieved I'd made it, I headed down the aisle in search of my seat. I stopped at my assigned row and, to my dismay, found I had the middle seat.

There are some things I don't do. Middle seats head my "No way, I ain't gonna!" list. My mood swing went from "I'm so grateful I caught my plane" to "I don't care what this ticket says, I'm not sitting in that center seat!"

I glanced around and realized, however, that this was the last available seat on the flight, and I would sit there or on the wing. I prayed for an attitude adjustment. I remembered that God will operate on our attitudes but that He requires us to cooperate.

CHAPTER ONE: *Hugs Are Gifts . . .*

To do my part, I tried to think of a way to make this irritating situation fun. Then it came to me that I could pretend I was Oprah Winfrey and my seat partners were my guests. I would interview them. Now, this had possibilities!

I turned my interview efforts toward the man sitting next to me. I had already observed something about this young man when I was being seated. He called me "Ma'am." At the time I thought, *He must be in the service,* so I asked, "You in the service?"

"Yes, ma'am, I am. The marines."

"Hey, Marine, where are you coming from?"

"The Desert Storm, ma'am."

"No kidding? How long were you there?" I continued.

"A year and a half. I'm on my way home. My family will be at the airport. I'm so scared." As he said this last sentence, he took in a short, nervous breath.

"Scared? Of what?" I asked.

"Oh, all this hero stuff. I'm not a hero, I'm just me, and I don't want my family to be disappointed."

"Take it from me, Marine, your parents just want you to come home safe."

Then Michael told me that when he lived at home, he and his mother were friends. When he joined the service and was stationed in Hawaii, they had written to each other and had become good friends. But when he went to Desert Storm, they became best friends.

"She will never know how she affected my life while I was away," he continued. "I've never thought of myself as a religious person, but while I was in the Storm, I learned to pray. The example I followed was the one my mom set for me when I was growing up."

"What was the most difficult time for you?" I inquired in Oprah fashion.

"There was a four-month space when we had not seen a woman or a child. The day we drove into Kuwait was very emotional for us. The women stood in doorways, waving, but even more moving was when the children ran to greet us. Since I've been stateside waiting to go home, I've been thinking about my nephews, and I can hardly wait to hear them call me Uncle Michael. The title *uncle* means even more to me than being called *sergeant*."

About that time, the flight attendant was passing by, and I tugged at her skirt. She looked down, and I said, "Know what? He is returning from Desert Storm."

The attendant asked him several questions and then requested that he write his name on a piece of paper. Taking his signature, she headed toward the front of the plane.

Moments later, the pilot came on the intercom and said, "It has been brought to my attention that we have a VIP aboard. He is a returning GI from Desert Storm and is in seat 12F. As a representative of this airline and citizen of the United States of America, I salute you, Michael, and thank you for a job well done."

At that point, the entire plane burst into applause.

The pilot came back on and said, "We are making our final approach into the Detroit Metro Airport."

Michael's breath caught.

I looked up and saw his eyes had filled with tears. He peeked through a tear to see if I had noticed, and of course there I was, goggling at him.

He said softly, "I just don't want to cry."

"It's okay," I told him. "I checked a marine manual on this one, and it's all right to cry. Some of the most admirable men I've ever known have shed tears at appropriate times, and Michael, this is a right time."

"Then you don't think I need to blame this on my contacts," he responded grinning.

"I don't think so," I said with a giggle.

As our plane taxied in, I told him the best gift my son brought me when he returned from eighteen months in Guam was that after he made his way through the waiting crowd, he scooped me up in his arms and held me for a very long time.

It was time to deplane, and when Michael stood, the men all around us slapped him on the back and pumped his arm, thanking him for his contribution.

MIDDLE MAN

Michael's homecoming included a lineup of relatives armed with video equipment, flags, cameras, and banners. When we were close enough for eyes to focus in and distinguish which one was Michael, his family began to chant, "Michael, Michael, Michael."

Even from a distance, I could identify his mom. She was the one leaping the highest in the air. A guard leaned against the wall, watching to make sure no one stepped over the security line. But every time Michael's mom jumped into the air, she came down with her toe just over the line to let the guard know who was really in charge.

When Michael stood, the men all around us slapped him on the back and pumped his arm, thanking him for his contribution.

As we got closer, she stopped jumping, and her hands went over her mouth to muffle the building sobs. Tears poured down her arms and dropped off her elbows . . . just over the line.

I gave him a final nudge toward his family, and they engulfed him, everyone in tears. I saw Michael find his mom in the crowd and pull her into his arms and hold her for a very long time.

When we got to the baggage-claim area, I prayed for the first time ever that my luggage would be delayed. Before long, the whole Desert Storm entourage came down to claim Michael's duffel bags.

Michael was still surrounded by family when I saw a youngster toddle over and pull on his pant leg. I realized this must be one of the nephews he was so eager to see again. When I noticed how young the boy was and remembered Michael had been gone for a year and a half, I held my breath to watch how the boy would react to his uncle.

Michael's face lit up as he reached down and picked up the young boy. His nephew wrapped his chubby legs around the sergeant's waist, and his arms encircled Michael's neck. Then the boy's mom came over, and I heard her ask, "Honey, who's got you?"

He looked up, his young eyes reflecting his hero, and said, "Uncle Michael."

I could breathe again.

A few minutes later, the thought hit me that I almost missed being a part of this tender event because I hadn't wanted to sit in the middle.

STITCHES IN TIME

Philip Gulley

Electricity was discovered by the ancient Greeks, though it didn't find its way to my in-laws' farm until the summer of 1948. That's when the truck from the Orange County Rural Electric Cooperative made its way down Grimes Lake Road, planting poles and stringing wire. My mother-in-law, Ruby, sat on her front porch snapping beans while the linemen set the poles. That night she asked her husband, Howard, what he thought of her getting an electric sewing machine. Her treadle sewing machine was broken, the victim of two high-spirited boys who had pumped the treadle to an early death.

They drove to Bedford the next day to the Singer Sewing Center and bought a brand-new electric Singer with a buttonholer, a cabinet, and a chair. It cost two hundred and forty dollars, money they'd earned from selling a truckload of hogs to the meatpacking plant in New Solsberry.

CHAPTER ONE: *Hugs Are Gifts . . .*

Ruby set into sewing for her boys. They added three children to their flock. More sewing. After supper, when the table was cleared and dishes washed, Ruby would bend over the machine, churning out clothes for her children and her neighbors. Thousands of dresses and shirts and pants. Clothes for dolls. Clothes for the minister's wife in town. Prom dresses. Wedding dresses. The Singer raised its needle millions of times. Her family would fall asleep under Ruby-made quilts, lulled to sleep by the Singer's hum.

The kids grew up and moved away. Grandchildren came, eight in all. The Singer stitched maternity clothes, baby dresses, baptismal gowns, and quilts for the cribs. In 1987, Ruby called us on the phone, discouraged. After thirty-nine years, her Singer was limping. She took it to Mr. Gardner in the next town over. He fixed sewing machines but couldn't revive hers. He sent it away to Chicago. A month later it came back, a paper tag hanging from its cord. *Obsolete. Parts not available*, the tag read.

I went to a sewing machine store the next day to buy a new one. Her old one was metal. The new machines are plastic and have computers and cost the same as Ruby's first car. They give classes on how to use them. In the display window was a 1948 metal Singer blackhead.

"Does that one work?" I asked the man.

"I don't know," he said. "Let's plug it in." He plugged it in. It hummed to life.

"It's not for sale," he told me. "It's a display. There aren't a lot of these old Singer blackheads around anymore."

I told him about Ruby—how she lives by herself and sews to keep busy, how she only charges six dollars to make a dress because the people she sews for don't have a lot of money, how a lot of times she doesn't charge a dime, how sewing is her ministry.

He sold the machine to me for twenty-five dollars.

The next weekend we hauled it down to Ruby's. She was sitting on the front porch, watching for our car to round the corner on the gravel lane. She came outside and stood by the car as we opened the trunk. As she peered down at the '48 blackhead, a smile creased her face.

"It's just like my old one," she whispered.

We plugged the old Singer in . . . When Ruby heard the hum she clapped her hands.

We wrestled it inside and installed it in her old cabinet. Perfect fit. Plugged it in. When Ruby heard the hum, she clapped her hands.

It's still going strong. Ruby still charges six dollars a dress—unless it's a bride's dress; then she sews it by hand. That'll cost you fifteen dollars, but only if you can afford it.

Ruby travels north to visit her granddaughter Rachael. Rachael shows Ruby her Barbie doll, then asks Ruby if she could maybe please sew some clothes for Barbie. The first night Ruby is home, she bends over her '48 blackhead, stitching matching dresses for Rachael and her Barbie. Way past midnight she sews. The next morning she drives to town and mails a package northward. Three days later the phone rings. It's Rachael calling to say "Thank you" and "I love you" and "When can I see you again?"

On two other occasions, my wife and I found 1948 Singer blackheads in antique stores. We bought them and gave them to Ruby. She's got a lot of sewing ahead, and we don't want her to run out of sewing machines before she runs out of things to sew.

I don't always applaud every new thing that comes down the road, though I'm grateful that in 1948 electricity made its way down the Grimes Lake Road. I'm grateful, too, for a woman who sews way into the night, who dispenses love one stitch at a time.

THAT'S WHAT FRIENDS DO

T. Suzanne Eller

Jack tossed the papers on my desk, his eyebrows knit into a straight line as he glared at me.

"What's wrong?" I asked.

He jabbed a finger at the proposal. "Next time you want to change anything, ask me first," he said, turning on his heels and leaving me stewing in anger. *How dare he treat me like that*, I thought. I had changed one long sentence and corrected grammar—something I thought I was paid to do.

It's not that I hadn't been warned. The women who had served in my place before me called him names I couldn't repeat. One coworker took me aside the first day. "He's personally responsible for two different secretaries leaving the firm," she whispered.

As the weeks went by, I grew to despise Jack. It was against everything I believed in—turn the other cheek and love your enemies. But Jack quickly slapped a verbal insult on any cheek

13

turned his way. I prayed about it, but to be honest, I wanted to put him in his place, not love him.

One day, another of his episodes left me in tears. I stormed into his office, prepared to lose my job if needed, but not before I let the man know how I felt. I opened the door and Jack glanced up.

"What?" he said abruptly.

Suddenly I knew what I had to do. After all, he deserved it.

I sat across from him. "Jack, the way you've been treating me is wrong. I've never had anyone speak to me that way. As a professional, it's wrong, and it's wrong for me to allow it to continue," I said. Jack snickered nervously and leaned back in his chair. I closed my eyes briefly. *God help me*, I prayed.

> *"I want to make you a promise. I will be a friend," I said.*

"I want to make you a promise. I will be a friend," I said. "I will treat you as you deserve to be treated, with respect and kindness. You deserve that," I said. "Everybody does." I slipped out of the chair and closed the door behind me.

Jack avoided me the rest of the week. Proposals, specs, and letters appeared on my desk while I was at lunch, and the corrected versions were not seen again. I brought cookies to the office one day and left a batch on Jack's desk. Another day I left a note. "Hope your day is going great," it read. Over the next few weeks, Jack reappeared. He was reserved, but there were no other episodes.

Coworkers cornered me in the break room. "Guess you got to Jack," they said. "You must have told him off good." I shook my head.

"Jack and I are becoming friends," I said in faith. I refused to talk about him. Every time I saw Jack in the hall, I smiled at him. After all, that's what friends do.

One year after our "talk," I discovered I had breast cancer. I was thirty-two, the mother of three beautiful young children, and scared. The cancer had metastasized to my lymph nodes, and the statistics were not great for long-term survival. After surgery, I visited with friends and loved ones who tried to find the right words. No one knew what to say. Many said the wrong things. Others wept, and I tried to encourage them. I clung to hope.

The last day of my hospital stay, the door darkened and Jack stood awkwardly on the threshold. I waved him in with a smile, and he walked over to my bed. Without a word, he placed a bundle beside me. Inside lay several bulbs.

"Tulips," he said.

I smiled, not understanding.

He cleared his throat. "If you plant them when you get home, they'll come up next spring." He shuffled his feet. "I just wanted you to know that I think you'll be there to see them when they come up."

Tears clouded my eyes, and I reached out my hand.

"Thank you," I whispered.

Jack grasped my hand and gruffly replied, "You're welcome. You can't see it now, but next spring you'll see the colors I picked out for you." He turned and left without a word.

I have seen those red-and-white-striped tulips push through the soil every spring for over ten years now. In fact, this September the doctor will declare me cured. I've seen my children graduate from high school and enter college. In a moment when I prayed for just the right word, a man with very few words said all the right things.

After all, that's what friends do.

YOU DID THIS FOR ME?

Max Lucado

He deserves our compassion. When you see him, do not laugh. Do not mock. Do not turn away or shake your head. Just gently lead him to the nearest bench and help him sit down.

Have pity on the man. He is so fearful, so wide-eyed. He's a deer on the streets of Manhattan. Tarzan walking through the urban jungle. He's a beached whale, wondering how he got here and how he'll get out.

Who is this forlorn creature? This ashen-faced orphan? He is—please remove your hats out of respect—he is the man in the women's department. Looking for a gift.

The season may be Christmas. The occasion may be her birthday or their anniversary. Whatever the motive, he has come out of hiding. Leaving behind his familiar habitat of sporting good stores, food courts, and the big-screen television in the appliance department, he ventures into the unknown world of women's wear. You'll spot him easily. He's the motionless one in the aisle. Were it not for the sweat rings under his arms, you'd think he was a mannequin.

But he isn't. He is a man in a woman's world, and he's never seen so much underwear. At the Wal-Mart where he buys his, it's all wrapped up and fits on one shelf. But here he is in a forest of lace. His father warned him about places like this. Though the sign above says "linger-ie," he knows he shouldn't.

So he moves on, but he doesn't know where to go. You see, not every man has been prepared for this moment as I was. My father saw the challenge of shopping for women as a rite of passage, right in there with birds and bees and tying neckties. He taught my brother and me how to survive when we shopped. I can remember the day he sat us down and taught us two words. To get around in a foreign country, you need to know the language, and my father taught us the language of the ladies' department.

"There will come a time," he said solemnly, "when a salesperson will offer to help you. At that moment take a deep breath and say this phrase, 'Es-tée Lau-der.'" On every gift-giving occasion for years after, my mom received three gifts from the three men in her life: Estée Lauder, Estée Lauder, and Estée Lauder.

My fear of the women's department was gone. But then I met Denalyn. Denalyn doesn't like Estée Lauder. Though I told her it made her smell motherly, she didn't change her mind. I've been in a bind ever since.

This year for her birthday I opted to buy her a new dress. When the salesperson asked me Denalyn's size, I said I didn't know. I honestly don't. I know I can wrap my arm around her and that her hand fits nicely in mine. But her dress size? I never inquired. There are certain questions a man doesn't ask.

The woman tried to be helpful. "How does she compare to me?" Now, I was taught to be polite to women, but I couldn't be polite and answer the question. There was only one answer, "She is thinner."

I stared at my feet, looking for a reply. After all, I write books. Surely I could think of the right words. I considered being direct: "She is less of you."

Or complimentary: "You are more of a woman than she is."

Perhaps a hint would suffice? "I hear the store is downsizing."

Finally I swallowed and said the only think I knew to say, "Estée Lauder."

She pointed me in the direction of the perfume department, but I knew better than to enter. I would try the purses. Thought it would be easy. What could be complicated about selecting a tool for holding cards and money? I've used the same money clip for eight years. What would be difficult about buying a purse?

Oh, naive soul that I am. Tell an attendant in the men's

department that you want a wallet, and you are taken to a small counter next to the cash register. Your only decision is black or brown. Tell an attendant in the ladies' department that you want a purse, and you are escorted to a room. A room of shelves. Shelves with purses. Purses with price tags. Small but potent price tags . . . prices so potent they should remove the need for a purse, right?

I was pondering this thought when the salesperson asked me some questions. Questions for which I had no answer. "What kind of purse would your wife like?" My blank look told her I was clueless, so she began listing the options: "Handbag? shoulder bag? glove bag? backpack? shoulder pack? change purse?"

Dizzied by the options, I had to sit down and put my head between my knees lest I faint. Didn't stop her. Leaning over me, she continued, "Moneybag? tote bag? pocketbook? satchel?"

"Satchel?" I perked up at the sound of a familiar word. Satchel Paige pitched in the major leagues. This must be the answer. I straightened my shoulders and said proudly, "Satchel."

Apparently she didn't like my answer. She began to curse at me in a foreign language. Forgive me for relating her vulgarity, but she was very crude. I didn't understand all she said, but I do know she called me a "Dooney Bird" and threatened to "brighten" me with a spade that belonged to someone named Kate. When she laid claim to "our mawny," I put my hand over the wallet in my hip pocket and defied, "No, it's my money." That was enough. I got out of there as fast as I could. But as I left the room, I gave her a bit of her own medicine. "Estée Lauder!" I shouted and ran as fast as I could.

Oh, the things we do to give gifts to those we love.

But we don't mind, do we? We would do it all again. Fact is, we do it all again. Every Christmas, every birthday, every so often we find ourselves in foreign territory. Grownups are in toy stores, dads are in teen stores. Wives are in the hunting department, and husbands are in the purse department.

Not only do we enter unusual places, we do unusual things. We assemble bicycles at midnight. We hide the new tires with mag wheels under the stairs. One fellow I heard about rented a movie theater so he and his wife could see their wedding pictures on their anniversary.

> *Oh, the things we do to give gifts to those we love.*

And we'd do it all again. Having pressed the grapes of service, we drink life's sweetest wine—the wine of giving. We are at our best when we are giving. In fact, we are most like God when we are giving.

UNEXPECTED GIFTS

Nance Guilmartin

hree women are standing in line waiting to order at one of those fashionable upscale restaurants where you can get fabulous French cooking at a cafeteria bistro. Out of the blue, a gentleman comes up and says to one of them, the tall, elegant, soft-spoken, sparkly-eyed blonde, "Excuse me, I just have to tell you, you are so beautiful." Then he walks away.

The other two ladies are delighted. They giggle and stifle a whoop because they've been telling their friend for years how beautiful she is. But Elisabeth doesn't believe them. She discounts their compliments and sees herself as not particularly attractive. Her reaction to the man's attention was to blush and to be embarrassed.

They're again standing in line waiting to pick up their orders when the guy comes back and says the same thing to Elisabeth: "I just have to tell you again, you are soooo beautiful." And he walks away.

Unexpected Gifts

By now Elisabeth is really embarrassed. She went out today without even putting on any makeup—not something that a well-trained Southern woman ordinarily does. But today isn't an ordinary day. Putting on her face wasn't high on her to-do list this morning when she took Ron, her beloved husband of thirty-three years, for his first chemotherapy treatment. The supposedly benign tumor he'd had removed the month before had, to their astonishment, turned out to be cancerous, and everything had changed.

Today she is with her best buddies for some moral support after having been with her husband at the hospital. It was a ladies' lunch break. And during the lunch they finally are eating, the same guy shows up a third time. Only this time he doesn't walk away. He wants to make sure that this beautiful woman doesn't think he is trying to hit on her. Flirt maybe, but that wasn't even the point of his comments to her. He explains himself in a way that suddenly makes each of the wary women give him their complete attention.

"You see," he tells them, "I've been diagnosed with an inoperable brain tumor. It has spread everywhere, and I don't have long to live. These days, I just say what I want, when I want. And you are beautiful, and I wanted you to know it. I'm sorry if I've embarrassed you, but life is so short, and I wasn't going to sit there and ignore what my heart told me to say."

Each of the women has tears in her eyes as he speaks his truth to them. Slowly Elisabeth starts telling her story to this man, who moments ago had been a stranger she was afraid of and was ready to avoid. She tells him about her husband. About their determination to fight the colon cancer. As luck, or fate, or more than coincidence would have it, this stranger is a doctor, a brain surgeon. Upon hearing her story, he pauses to acknowledge that

Appreciating the unexpected takes practice.

his mind is working a little slower these days, as he gropes for the name and number of the cancer specialist he wants to give her. Eventually

he remembers it, writes it down, and hands her what could be a lifeline in her husband's battle.

The funny thing is that just a week earlier, this attractive, loving wife had told her friends that she was going to try living more in the present. She wanted to be less concerned about the future. To be less concerned about what people would think of her taking a leave of absence from her "very important" job to help her husband through this treatment. She wanted to see what life would be like if she just paid attention to the little moments, to the present.

Look what showed up on her plate at lunch with friends! Had she slipped into embarrassed avoidance or annoyed judgment, she might have driven away the gift of a dying man's determination to live his life, one beautiful moment at a time. Appreciating the unexpected takes practice. It takes a willingness to suspend judgment of another's motives and an openness to be with what is. Being with what is takes practice because it doesn't necessarily come naturally. Of course, you can exercise common sense and make sure your gut tells you the situation is safe. And if that's the case, then you can take a step toward being open, which means letting yourself be curious about what someone you don't know, who owes you nothing, is trying to give you for no apparent reason.

When things aren't going the way you'd planned in life, you definitely need your friends. You need to be able to laugh and to cry and to wonder why life has taken an unexpected turn. Sometimes, though, a stranger does come into your life—at a restaurant, on an airplane, in a hospital waiting room—and that stranger can offer you an extraordinary gift if you have the presence of mind and heart to be open to receiving it.

LITTLE CHAD

Dale Galloway

_L_ ittle Chad was a shy, quiet young fella. One day he came home and told his mother he'd like to make a valentine for everyone in his class. Her heart sank. She thought, "I wish he wouldn't do that!" because she had watched the children when they walked home from school. Her Chad was always behind them. They laughed and hung on to each other and talked to each other. But Chad was never included. Nevertheless, she decided she would go along with her son. So she purchased the paper and glue and crayons. For three whole weeks, night after night, Chad painstakingly made thirty-five valentines.

Valentine's Day dawned and Chad was beside himself with excitement! He carefully stacked them up, put them in a bag, and bolted out the door. His mom decided to bake him his favorite cookies and serve them up warm and nice with a cool glass of milk when he came home from school. She just knew he'd be disappointed; maybe that would ease the pain a little. It hurt her to think that he wouldn't get many valentines—maybe none at all.

That afternoon she had the cookies and milk out on the table. When she heard the children outside, she looked out the window. Sure enough here they came, laughing and

She had watched the children when they walked home from school. Her Chad was always behind them.

having the best time. And, as always, there was Chad in the rear. He walked a little faster than usual. She fully expected him to burst into tears as soon as he got inside. His arms were empty, she noticed, and when the door opened she choked back the tears.

"Mommy has some warm cookies and milk for you."

But he hardly heard her words. He just marched right on by, his face aglow, and all he could say was:

"Not a one . . . not a one."

Her heart sank.

And then he added, "I didn't forget a one, not a single one!"

CHAPTER TWO

---

*Hugs Teach Lessons
from the Heart*

It is only with the heart that one can see rightly; what is essential is invisible to the eye.

ANTOINE DE SAINT-EXUPERY

Personal Testimony

Nika Maples

*D*ream: to replace Diane Sawyer on *Prime Time Live*."

I am smiling beside those words in my high-school yearbook. I was absolutely sure where I was going then. After being elected Most Likely to Succeed, I knew that my friends were sure too.

University journalism courses were a thrill. By my sophomore year in college, I was volunteering at the campus radio station and writing for the school newspaper. I laughed with friends over countless cafeteria dinners when, inevitably, someone would turn on the television set across the room. The evening news turned my head. *That is going to be me*, I thought. *That is going to be me someday.*

Late-breaking news flash.

"Excuse me," Jehovah said, tapping me on a cold shoulder. "May I have your attention, please?"

I have loved God, worshiped him, from my first memories of

singing "Blue Skies and Rainbows" in Vacation Bible School. I have not always, however, actively sought his will in the decisions of my life, whether major or minor. I have not always listened and waited for his voice.

Elijah heard deity in a gentle whisper when he was still enough to listen. *Why couldn't God have spoken up a bit?* I have mused on occasion. Apparently, his servant's stillness was the integral factor in God's being heard. Elijah had to be quiet.

"Be still," God said to me. I blustered on in my sophomoric storm.

"Be still."

I was a member of a social club. I waited tables at a local Italian restaurant. I had a small part in an annual variety show. I spent my free time with my boyfriend. I juggled eighteen hours of coursework. There was the radio station. There was the newspaper. There was church. My storm became a category four hurricane, and I could not hear God.

"Peace. Be still," he insisted. "Be still."

And I was.

Six weeks after my twentieth birthday, I suddenly fell to my face on the carpet of my bedroom, unable to move. Lupus, an autoimmune disorder, had caused a massive brain injury. In the time it takes to turn a radio dial, I became a quadriplegic. Just the week before, I had purchased new running shoes.

PERSONAL TESTIMONY

In the intensive-care unit, I overheard physicians warning of the worst: I may have as few as forty-eight hours left to live. Dear friends and family clung to my quiet hands, caressing limp fingers and offering disbelieving good-byes. I felt their tears fall on my arms and run down my wrists. Conscious, I would mark the passage of time by the regularity of my heart monitor. I could not speak. I could not open my eyes.

This is suffering, I declared. *This is suffering*, I said to God. I talked to him and him alone, day after excruciating day. I continually asked my only Friend, why?

"I consider that [your] present sufferings are not worth comparing with the glory that will be revealed in [you]," he answered (Romans 8:18).

I had memorized that verse in seventh-grade Bible class, not knowing what it meant. What did I understand of glory then? What did I know of suffering? I had tucked the verse away in my heart. God was packing my spiritual suitcase for a journey across the valley of the shadow of death. When those words resurfaced, I was quiet and ready to hear his whisper.

"Not worth comparing," he said as he came close.

"Not worth comparing." The words felt like breath on the back of my neck.

"Not worth comparing," I began to say as weeks passed.

My radio frequency finally was tuned in to God, and I listened.

CHAPTER TWO: *Hugs Teach Lessons* . . .

Acquaintance with suffering intensified; the characteristics of glory ever deepened in mystery.

Him. Glory is God himself. Glory revealed in us is not so much the hope of heaven or miracles wondrously unfurled in our lives, but the majesty of the moment when our suffering quiets us into submission, and we realize that the Creator deigns to live inside the created. We, who are a little hard of hearing, have a front-row seat at the symphony.

My future, my destiny, I have discovered, never was a successful career, but him. My purpose is God. I live, I am, and yes, I move, for him.

> *Amid the rain and ruin, I was at peace for the first time. In the center, I was still.*

At one time, every dream I had treasured was irreparably broken. Storm wreckage. But amid the rain and ruin, I was at peace for the first time. In the center, I was still.

A decade now distances me from those early hospital days, and doctors are astonished by my recovery. After months of grueling speech and physical therapy, I eventually regained the ability to speak well and to walk with a prominent limp and a cane. My youthful dreams of delivering the nightly news are all but abandoned. It is a greater honor to deliver the good news around the world. I have shared the story of God's glory displayed in my life in countries such as Japan, Australia, Germany, Canada, and Thailand. I even taught the children of missionaries in Bangkok for almost a year.

My dearest ministry today is teaching in a public high school. I earned my degree in journalism after all, and I use it to teach English, photojournalism, and creative writing. On the first day of school, I always tell my students about the day I fell to the carpet, so many years ago. Mouths gape, eyes widen, and teenagers sit enrapt; they cannot believe how far I have come. I pray often that my example shines with the likeness of Christ, even though they may not hear the fullness of my testimony in English class.

Mirroring God has become my career plan, my life goal. Sometimes I look into the sweet faces of my students, while reminding them that life can be lost in a moment, and I am overwhelmed with blessing. A God-centered life is the highest call for living, and I would not want to be living anything less.

An Awesome Deal

Katherine Grace Bond

I was walking past Jake's Vintage Usables and Collectibles just like every day on my way home from my friend Jeremy's. Couldn't see anything to buy in the window that day; it was all the same stuff as the day before.

Mr. Jake waved as he heard the bell jingle. "Eric, my boy!" Mr. Jake is older than my grandpa and nobody knows his last name. He's practically hairless and his face is full of creases. He always looks like he's thinking of something funny. Even his ears smile at the sides of his head. "So, what's black and white and red all over?" he challenged.

"A newspaper and . . . a sunburned zebra!"

"Ha!" Haven't stumped you yet."

"Anything new today?"

"Have a look." He winked and began cleaning a display case.

An Awesome Deal

The shop had a good kind of moldy smell. I rummaged through bins of antique postcards and faded comic books. There was an old Captain Zappo that looked okay. I tucked it under my arm. Then something on the wall caught my eye. I didn't have a clock, really, just my radio alarm, but it wasn't a cat with a tail that moved back and forth like this one. The eyes swung from side to side, as if they were hunting for a mouse. I had to buy it.

I looked at the sticker on the back. It was a good deal, an awesome deal. There was enough in my wallet. Friday is allowance day, and I can do whatever I want with it. I should set aside ten percent for the collection plate, and I really am going to—it's just that there's a lot of stuff I need. Besides, my allowance is the same amount as last year. A kid my age really should get more.

Mr. Jake put the clock and the comic book in a bag and gave me my change. He saluted, making me smile. "Be strong and courageous, my boy!"

I slid the coins into my pocket and they jingled as I walked to the door, looking around one last time to see if there was anything else I needed. There wasn't, so on the way home I stopped at Quik-Mart and got some Mondo Bubble.

The clock fit over my dresser, right above the bike headlight I'd bought the day before, and my baseball cards. I needed a clock like that.

CHAPTER TWO: *Hugs Teach Lessons* . . .

Before dinner, Mom took me into town with her to check out the sales. I asked her if we could buzz past Gregg's Greenlake Cycle on Woodlawn, just to look.

"Mom, stop the car!"

Right smack in the center of the window was the most awesome skateboard I had ever seen. It was a pro-board: twin-tipped, low to the ground, 42-millimeter wheels. This was no banana board.

"Will you get it for me?"

Mom rolled her eyes. "Eric, you already have a skateboard."

"But, Mom, it's three years old! It glows in the dark. The kids laugh at it. And look, it's an awesome deal."

"Good, then use your birthday money from Grandma."

"It's . . . gone. I used it for baseball cards."

She shook her head. "Well, I guess you'll just have to save up."

"Save up? How?"

"There's always the garage."

Mom had been trying to get me to clean her garage all summer. Suddenly I wanted to do it. I also did the flower beds, the fence and the windows. It would take a few weeks, but it'd be worth it.

It was hard to pass up Mr. Jake's store. After a few days, he came out and waved.

"Eric, my boy! What's black and white and red all over?"

"A . . . newspaper and a skunk with a diaper rash."

AN AWESOME DEAL

"Ha! Haven't seen much of you lately, strong and courageous one." He seemed older today.

"Oh, well I've been, um, busy, you know?"

Mr. Jake nodded and winked and went back into his shop. After that I took a different route home. The money in my skateboard jar was adding up.

One Friday I did stop at Mr. Jake's store. Just to look, I told myself. When I turned the old brass doorknob, though, it was locked. Then I saw the orange "closed" sign.

"Didn't you hear?" Jeremy called from across the street. "Mr. Jake had a heart attack. He just got home from the hospital."

I scribbled a note and slipped it through the mail slot. "A blushing panda," it said. "Be strong and courageous."

The next morning was Saturday. Before she left for work, Mom wrapped up a casserole.

"Now carry that dish carefully, Eric. Tell Mr. Jake it can be warmed up in the microwave as soon as he's ready to eat it."

When I knocked on Mr. Jake's door, he called me to come in. His voice was so thin, I barely heard him.

"Eric, my boy. Glad you could stop by!" His craggy face lit up. I'd never been in his house before. It must've been a hundred years old. The kitchen floor was covered with cracked, grey linoleum. Next to the kitchen, Mr. Jake was sitting up in bed. He seemed skinnier than usual, but maybe it was because he was still in his pajamas. I showed him the casserole, and his eyes seemed to mist up a little.

"Thank you, Eric. Thank your mother for me. She's a good woman."

The refrigerator was one of those short, white ones with the rounded corners and "Frigidaire" written across the front in chrome. I opened the door to put the casserole in. All that was inside was a carton of orange juice and some fuzzy bread. That was it. Mr. Jake wasn't

I didn't want to be nosy, but I opened his cupboard doors, one by one.

watching. I didn't want to be nosy, but I opened his cupboard doors one by one. In the first cupboard were a few mismatched dishes, pots and pans, and cups in all sizes. In the next were a cake mix, a can of sardines and some oatmeal. The rest of the cupboards were empty.

We played checkers while he drank a glass of orange juice. He offered some to me, but I said no thank you. When he said good-bye, his voice didn't sound quite as thin.

At home I emptied the money out of my skateboard jar and counted it just as I did every day. There was a little more than enough and today was the day. I thought about those narrow wheels and the feel of the rough pavement under them. My mind invented new jumps and turns. The money filled my two hands, and coins slipped out between my fingers. I made it into a little pile.

There was this funny feeling in my chest, though. I remembered the cake mix and the sardines. I took 10 percent of the money out of the pile and set it aside for Sunday. There must be a lot of Mr. Jakes.

There was just enough left. I put it in my wallet and threw on my jacket. I was going to ride the board back so Jeremy could see it.

I walked past Mr. Jake's store. A few blocks ahead were the painted bicycles on the wall of Gregg's Greenlake Cycle. The wallet bulged in my back pocket.

At the corner I had to wait for the light. Roasting turkey smells came from the supermarket deli. I wondered if Mr. Jake had eaten Mom's casserole yet. The sign flashed red at me, "Joe's Super Foods."

The light changed. I only had ten seconds to cross this street. The cars waited at the crosswalk as my light turned yellow, then red. I turned away from the curb and walked into Joe's.

I filled the cart with pears, baked beans, cans of tuna, milk, and bread. I even bought a chicken. Maybe I could help him cook it.

The clerk rang up the sale and I slid my money across the counter. It was a good deal; an awesome deal.

POWER OF THE POWERLESS

Christopher de Vinck

I grew up in the house where my brother was on his back in
his bed for almost thirty-three years, in the same corner of
his room, under the same window, beside the same yellow walls.
Oliver was blind, mute. His legs were twisted. He didn't have the
strength to lift his head nor the intelligence to learn anything.

Today I am an English teacher, and each time I introduce my
class to the play about Helen Keller, "The Miracle Worker," I tell my
students about Oliver. One day, during my first year teaching, a boy
in the last row raised his hand and said, "Oh, Mr. de Vinck. You mean
he was a vegetable."

I stammered for a few seconds. My family and I fed Oliver.
We changed his diapers, hung his clothes and bed linen on the
basement line in winter, and spread them out white and clean on
the lawn in the summer. I always liked to watch the grasshoppers
jump on the pillowcases.

POWER OF THE POWERLESS

We bathed Oliver. Tickled his chest to make him laugh. Sometimes we left the radio on in his room. We pulled the shade down over his bed in the morning to keep the sun from burning his tender skin. We listened to him laugh as we watched television downstairs. We listened to him rock his arms up and down to make the bed squeak. We listened to him cough in the middle of the night.

"Well, I guess you could call him a vegetable. I called him Oliver, my brother. You would have liked him."

One October day in 1946, when my mother was pregnant with Oliver, her second son, she was overcome by fumes from a leaking coal-burning stove. My oldest brother was sleeping in his crib, which was quite high off the ground so the gas didn't affect him. My father pulled them outside, where my mother revived quickly.

On April 20, 1947, Oliver was born. A healthy looking, plump, beautiful boy. One afternoon, a few months later, my mother brought Oliver to a window. She held him there in the sun, the bright good sun, and there Oliver looked and looked directly into the sunlight, which was the first moment my mother realized that Oliver was blind.

My parents, the true heroes of this story, learned with the passing months, that blindness was only part of the problem. So they brought Oliver to Mt. Sinai Hospital in New York for tests to determine the extent of his condition.

The doctor said that he wanted to make it very clear to both my mother and father that there was absolutely nothing that could be done for Oliver. He didn't want my parents to grasp at false hope. "You could place him in an institution," he said. "But," my parents replied, "he is our son. We will take Oliver home, of course." The good doctor answered, "Then take him home and love him."

> *Oliver still remains the weakest, most helpless human being I ever met, and yet he was one of the most powerful human beings I ever met.*

Oliver grew to the size of a ten-year-old. He had a big chest, a large head. His hands and feet were those of a five-year-old, small and soft. We'd wrap a box of baby cereal for him at Christmas and place it under the tree; pat his head with a damp cloth in the middle of a July heat wave. His baptismal certificate hung on the wall above his head. A bishop came to the house and confirmed him.

Even now, years after his death from pneumonia on March 12, 1980, Oliver still remains the weakest, most helpless human being I ever met, and yet he was one of the most powerful human beings I ever met. He could do absolutely nothing except breathe, sleep, eat, and yet he was responsible for action, love, courage, insight.

When I was small my mother would say, "Isn't it wonderful that you can see?" And once she said, "When you go to heaven, Oliver will run to you, embrace you, and the first thing he will say is 'Thank you.'" I remember, too, my mother explaining to me that we were blessed with Oliver in ways that were not clear to her at first.

So often parents are faced with a child who is severely retarded, but who is also hyperactive, demanding or wild, who needs constant care. So many people have little choice but to place their child in an institution. We were fortunate that Oliver didn't need us to be in his room all day. He never knew what his condition was. We were blessed with his presence, a true presence of peace.

In my early twenties I met a girl and fell in love. After a few months I brought her home to meet my family. When my mother went to prepare dinner, I asked the girl, "Would you like to see Oliver?" for I had told her about my brother. "No," she answered.

Soon after, I met Roe, a lovely girl. She asked me the names of my brothers and sisters. She loved children. I thought she was wonderful. I brought her home after a few months to meet my family. Soon it was time for me to feed Oliver. I remember sheepishly asking Roe if she'd like to see him. "Sure," she said.

I sat at Oliver's bedside as Roe watched over my shoulder. I gave him his first spoonful, his second. "Can I do that?" Roe asked with ease, with freedom, with compassion, so I gave her the bowl and she fed Oliver one spoonful at a time.

The power of the powerless. Which girl would you marry? Today Roe and I have three children.

DANCE OF THE BLUE BUTTERFLY

Cathy Lee Phillips

*W*hen it happens, will you find a way to let me know you are okay?"

She was fifty-two years old, and after a sixteen-year battle with a horrible disease, her life was ending. Marked with the scars and bruises of prolonged medical treatment, her body was too weak to sustain life much longer. But she was very much alive at that moment, and in an ordinary room at Emory University Hospital in Atlanta, she wanted to talk—about life and death and faith, the things that are really important at such a time. I sat on the edge of the bed and held my mother's hand as we talked and laughed and cried.

"Nothing flashy. No lightning bolts or earthquakes." My request was not made in jest. It was a statement of faith. I believed fully in life after death—in her life after her death. I wanted, perhaps, to strengthen her with my confidence. At the same time, I wanted my faith to comfort me in that frightening moment.

"Just a simple sign," I continued, "one that will let me know that God is taking good care of you."

"I will," she quietly promised.

We continued our conversation, sharing the ordinary and the profound, the frustrations of the day, the mysteries of the universe, private jokes, and an appropriate touch of gossip. In the long run, we shared far more laughter than tears.

My mother had been desperately ill for sixteen years. In fact, there were times I could barely remember what my mother was like before the disease. Most days, in fact, I felt more intimately acquainted with Wegener's Granulomatosis, her rare and gruesome disease, than with my mother herself. Her appearance had dramatically changed. Her personality had been forever altered. Yet the pain of those sixteen years did not matter that afternoon in her hospital room. All that mattered was the moment and those matters of life and death and faith—and my question.

"When it happens, will you find a way to let me know you are okay?"

"I will," she promised.

A few days later, in the early hours of an August morning, my mother left behind her broken body and journeyed into her new life. I celebrated for her, secure in the faith that only her diseased body had died. My mother lived on, I knew, pain-free and strong for the first time in many years.

At her request, my husband, Jerry, made preparations for her memorial service. He was not only her son-in-law; Jerry was her pastor as well. As Jerry planned, I prepared a bulletin that included an order of worship and a few words about my mother's life. Once the inside of the bulletin was complete, I searched for an appropriate cover page. I had an abundance of artwork—crosses and flowers, birds and sunrises, words of Scripture and comfort. Nothing, though, seemed appropriate. Sensing my indecision, Jerry made the choice for me.

"Use this butterfly," he stated, holding a plain black-and-white graphic.

"It is so ordinary," I said. I wished for a photograph of a huge, brilliant blue butterfly. Blue was my mother's favorite color, I recalled.

"Use the butterfly," Jerry stated again. "It is the Christian symbol of resurrection, of rebirth, of new life."

Yes, the butterfly would be appropriate. It seemed that my mother had spent sixteen long years in a dark cocoon. At her death, though, she had been released from her cocoon of disease into a wonderful new life. So, placing the butterfly prominently on the cover, I completed the bulletin.

Jerry and I visited the church early the next morning. As he arranged his Bible and notes on the pulpit, I placed the bulletins for the ushers to distribute. Having attended to all the details, it was time to leave the little country church to travel to the funeral home.

As we stepped toward the car, Jerry suddenly seized my hand. "Don't move, Cathy, and look quickly!" he whispered.

On the hood of our car stood a brilliant butterfly. It was a splendid, majestic creature. A strikingly beautiful blue butterfly, completely blue except for the black markings accenting its tiny body. With its wings open wide, the small creature strolled gracefully atop the car for several minutes. Even as we walked closer, the butterfly remained on the hood.

I was amazed! Don't butterflies normally fly away in fear? This blue butterfly, though, seemed at peace and completely unafraid. Jerry and I stood transfixed for what seemed an eternity before the blue butterfly calmly spread its wings and took flight.

Smiling and crying at once, I realized my mother had kept her promise.

We watched intently as, dipping and diving with the wind, it flew unrestrained into the sunlight. Jerry held me tightly as this miraculous affirmation of resurrection unfolded before us in the form of a tiny blue butterfly. So simple, yet so profound in its significance. My mother had finally escaped her cocoon and entered into a new life with Christ. I knew that beyond any doubt.

As mysterious and frightening as it is, death is certainly not the end of life. It is merely a gateway to eternity.

Smiling and crying at once, I realized my mother had kept her promise. I turned my thankful heart toward the butterfly. It gently flew into the August sky, waltzing and gliding with the breeze, dancing the dance of life.

THE STRANGER WITH A LIFE IN HIS LUGGAGE

Diana Booher

Y ou have a lot of trees back here," I said to Vernon one Sunday afternoon in his backyard after we'd been dating only a few months.

"Yep."

"I thought you were going to be moving shortly?"

"I probably will."

"So how long does it take them to grow—won't you be gone before they're big enough to give you any shade?"

"Probably. But somebody will enjoy them after I'm gone." He moved the hose to a new set of roots. "I always plant trees wherever I live."

"Hmm." Seemed like a waste of time to me. I enjoy gardening about as much as I love to scrub a dirty skillet.

"Did I tell you about the man who helped me set all these trees out?"

I shook my head, and he related the following story.

Vernon watched as the old man relished his fried chicken, occasionally dabbing at the corners of his mouth with his napkin. The mom-and-pop restaurant drew only locals, even for Sunday lunch. In his single days, Vernon often stopped there to grab a bite of lunch on his way home from church. It was the kind of place where the owners call you by name and remember that you like gravy on the side.

His battered suitcase under the table beside him, the elderly diner had apparently walked from the bus station across the street. Vernon noticed that the old man had finished his lunch but didn't seem to be in any hurry to leave. He lingered over his glass of water, simply watching other diners as they came and went, occasionally moving his suitcase from side to side to prevent people from tripping as they passed among the tightly arranged tables. He seemed amused by the children who were flying paper airplanes over their food as their parents coaxed them to eat. The twinkle in his eye seemed to reveal memories of family days gone by.

Always intrigued by people with stories to tell,

The Stranger with a Life in His Luggage

Vernon took his last swig of iced tea and said to the older man across the narrow aisle, "Are you visiting someone here in Kingwood?"

"No. Just passing through."

"Where are you from?"

"Philadelphia." He paused for a moment, as if to assess Vernon's real interest in his itinerary. Obviously deciding Vernon's interest was genuine, he elaborated. "My wife died a few weeks ago. Been married fifty-two years. Decided I needed a change. Got all my belongings here in this case." He patted the bent brown bag as if it were a collie. "Yeah, going out to live with my son."

That much information in such a brief exchange was just the kind of thing my husband, Vernon, needed to build a two-hour conversation. Although women are often said to have special antennas for collecting information, Vernon does an admirable job himself. The old man's response was one of those thumbnail sketches that wallop you up beside the head with the same kind of impact you sometimes get from a novel or a movie.

As Vernon later related the incident to me, I could hear a leftover hint of sadness in his voice when he explained, "So I asked the old man to come home with me for the afternoon."

"You—what? A total stranger?"

"He had nowhere else to go."

So that Sunday in the restaurant he had said to the old man dining at the next table, "Where's your son live?"

"He's out in San Diego—or somewhere near there. That's where he's meeting my bus."

"Nice place." Vernon finished his tea and started to get up to pay his check. "So are you going to walk around here and see a little of the city before you go? There're some great walking trails near here."

The old man shook his head.

"So what time does your bus leave?"

"Ten o'clock tonight."

"You've got to wait nine hours?"

"Bus is not the best way to travel, I guess. But it's cheap." The old man smiled, not at all bitterly.

"So why don't you come on home with me for the afternoon, and I'll bring you back to catch your bus at ten o'clock? That's too long for you to have to sit here and wait."

The old man seemed to search Vernon's face for sincerity. "I wouldn't want to impose. I could just sit here another couple hours and then mosey on back over to the bus station."

"No, that won't be comfortable. I don't live far away. Got a little garden. I wasn't planning on doing anything special—just planting a few trees. I could use some help."

The Stranger with a Life in His Luggage

The old man's face lit up. "Oh, now that—yeah, I could help you do that. I know about planting trees." And with that, he reached for his suitcase and followed Vernon out of the restaurant.

Once in the backyard, after Vernon had given him some of his own old work clothes to change into, the old man seemed much younger. "If you

Friendship may be more appropriately measured in intensity than longevity.

want some advice, I'd tell you to stagger those trees," he said as Vernon was about to dig the second hole.

"What do you mean?"

"Like this." The visitor took the extra shovel and began to mark the spots across the lawn. When he returned to where Vernon was standing, he told him the reason: "The roots don't crowd each other, and the resulting shade from the canopy will be wider."

"I see," Vernon said appreciatively. "Nobody ever told me that before. Makes sense. Let's do it then."

They set out nine trees before dark. In between, they spread their lives.

When they'd finished, Vernon showed him to the extra shower so he could clean up and change back into his traveling clothes. He took him out for dinner on the way back to the bus station for his ten o'clock departure. As they parted, they exchanged phone numbers and vowed to keep in touch.

But Vernon never heard from the man again.

Four years later, Vernon received a letter from the old man's son, telling him that his father had recently passed away. The letter said in part, "My father never stopped talking about you and your kindness to him that Sunday afternoon. He was truly amazed that in this day and time you would invite him, a stranger, into your home—and make him feel useful. That was the best part. I found your address in his room and thought I should let you know what your kindness meant to him. He talked of you and that day often, as if you were old friends."

As Vernon related the story to me while watering the saplings spread across his lawn, I understood that they had indeed been friends—even if for only a day. Friendship may be more appropriately measured in intensity than longevity.

In Jesus's words to his disciples I think he was making the same distinction that Vernon conveyed when he invited the old man to join him. "I no longer call you servants. . . . Instead, I have called you friends" (John 15:15). The distinction provides context and reason for those brief encounters along life's way.

PERFECT GIFT

Shelley Mickle

*Y*esterday I saw a child receive the perfect gift. I didn't expect to see it. He didn't expect to receive it. And it happened in the most unlikely place. It was on the airplane flying back from the horse show in Oklahoma. I was sitting beside this eight-year-old boy and his mother. Just as we started to come in for a landing, the heavens let loose with one of those gullywhopper thunderstorms. Lightning, rain, thunder—you know the kind—you begin to wonder if your affairs are enough in order to keep all your relatives from squabbling over whatever piddling stuff you leave.

We bounced around for a while, like one of those carnival rides I never had enough guts to buy a ticket for. Then the pilot came on over the microphone and said in his smooth-as-chewing-gum voice that it was just way too rough for him to try to set us down here, so he was just going to head on over to Jacksonville and set us down there.

CHAPTER TWO: *Hugs Teach Lessons* . . .

As soon as we flew out of the bad weather, and the plane stopped bucking, a low moan of complaint moved throughout the coach section. Not only did we now face another thirty-minute plane ride, but our relatives or friends, who had come to meet us, were standing down there on the ground being told we were a no-show. The plan was that a bus was being sent to pick us up at the other airport, then we'd have to ride it all the way back.

Looking at his mother's face, you would have thought he was telling her the most wonderful and hilarious tales she'd ever heard.

The boy sitting beside me was dressed in jeans and boots and a plaid shirt. He had a cowlick over his forehead like a hand of cards, and his mother was in shorts with a ruffled blouse.

They reminded me of people I had grown up with in the cotton belt in Arkansas. More than likely their lives moved to the rhythm of weather and crops, or maybe night shifts and overtime. When I asked them who would have been waiting for them, I learned that the boy's father had driven many miles to be at the airport. Our delay was a real bummer, we agreed. And the mother was a good bit distressed. It was then that the most amazing exchange took place.

While the rest of us ducked back into our magazines, or went on with grumbling about our inconvenience, the boy began telling his mother stories. I don't know what they were about, or where he got them, but looking at his mother's face, you would have thought he was telling her the most wonderful and hilarious tales she'd ever heard. She was laughing and watching him as if his every third sentence held a most delicious surprise. More than once, she reached over and touched him on his arm and cried out, "Stop, stop. I can't take it anymore," as if she were being tickled to death. The more teasingly she punched him, the more he talked on.

Throughout our whole ride, and even after we were taxiing on the runway into our detoured airport, the boy and his mother continued their interchange. When I got up to get my bag out of the overhead compartment, I glanced down at them. They weren't even aware that I'd been watching them. But the boy's mother was still grinning, and I could see that without a doubt the most wondrous light had been lit in that boy's face.

I'm pretty sure it's still there. In fact, I'm pretty convinced if anything lasts at all, it is this kind of light that is eternal.

I consider it a privilege to have been there when it was given.

CHAPTER THREE

—⊶⊷⊷⊶—

Hugs Show Love
from the Heart

Love's finest speech is

without words.

HADEWIJCK OF BRABANT

DWELLING IN GRACE

Britta Coleman

Zorro the new puppy is here. My daughter's dog looks like a miniature blue heeler, and he fits in the palm of my hand.

He doesn't know he's a little dog. He's 100 percent puppy, with all the chewing, jumping, leaping, eating and tinkling that indicates. He has the attention span of a gnat, plays until he crashes, and makes us frustrated and laugh all in the same breath.

In short, he's like a toddler.

I'd almost forgotten what it was like to have a little one in the house again. Almost. See, this morning I was on my couch doing my study and prayer time, trying to get quiet before the day unfolded. Hot coffee, fresh pen, and a still house after the children left for school. A perfect opportunity.

And then came Zorro. Cavorting on my lap. Chewing on my pen. Gnawing the corners of my cozy throw blanket.

David the psalmist wrote, "His delight is in the law of the LORD, and on his law he meditates day and night" (Psalm 1:2).

It's hard to meditate when a half-pound dog is wriggling with all his might, hoping to get a good lick at your ear.

Be gentle with yourself. Dwell in the grace given to you.

I actually prayed God would make Zorro quiet so I could focus.

Didn't happen.

It reminded me of when my children were small, when I longed to pursue deeper spirituality, but there wasn't enough time, or frankly, enough energy.

Babies are time consuming, and can be mentally and physically exhausting. It seemed every time I found stillness, instead of praying, I'd be asleep.

A friend of mine and I were talking about spiritual pursuits, and about seeking serenity. She commented, "You know, it's easy to be a monk and achieve peace. Live in the mountains, beautiful scenery, no kids, no interruptions. But a woman with three kids at home, peanut butter in her hair, and a baby on his third day of diarrhea—show me a woman like that who's halfway sane, and I'll show you a spiritual giant."

Good point.

I often look back on that young mom that I was, and here's

what I'd say to myself (and to all walking the difficult path that is being a mommy):

God is pleased with you. He has gifted you with children, and honored you with motherhood. He knows you are tired and weary. He knows your heart seeks to do what is right, even while your Bible grows dusty, or splattered with baby food or worse.

He understands those stolen moments of simply watching your child sleep, or resolutely tugging your husband's socks the right way out before you fold them, or your need to slip into a rare and wonderful bubble bath.

Shift your perspective: those things, those moments, can be worship. Be gentle with yourself. Dwell in the grace given to you.

Times and seasons change, and all too quickly at that.

Soak it all in, revel in the beauty of the moment. Even when that moment is a screaming toddler, a messy house, or a dream for yourself that must wait another year. And another.

Because all too soon the stages shift, and the rooms quiet and the floors stay clean and those sticky hands grow big and independent.

And you might one day forget how your heart yearned for a quiet moment.

Almost.

Yes, that's what I'd tell her—myself—that mother of years past.

And I keep her in my heart so I don't forget.

My season has changed, but God sends me reminders. Zorro, the toddler Chihuahua. I close my book and pick up this little fuzzball of love and nuzzle his baby face.

I remember.

THE PRINCE'S HAPPY HEART

A Folktale

*O*nce upon a time there was a little prince in a country far away from here. He was one of the happiest little princes who ever lived. All day long he laughed and sang and played. His voice was as sweet as music. His footsteps brought joy wherever he went. Everyone thought that this was due to magic. Hung about the prince's neck on a gold chain was a wonderful heart. It was made of gold and set with precious stones.

The godmother of the little prince had given the heart to him when he was very small. She had said as she slipped it over his curly head: "To wear this happy heart will keep the prince happy always. Be careful that he does not lose it."

All the people who took care of the little prince were very careful to see that the chain of the happy heart was clasped. But one day they found the little prince in his garden, very sad and sorrowful. His face was wrinkled into an ugly frown.

"Look!" he said, and he pointed to his neck. Then they saw what had happened.

The happy heart was gone. No one could find it, and each day the little prince grew more sorrowful. At last they missed him. He had gone, himself, to look for the lost happy heart that he needed so much.

The little prince searched all day. He looked in the city streets and along the country roads. He looked in the shops and in the doors of the houses where rich people lived. Nowhere could he find the heart that he had lost. At last it was almost night. He was very tired and hungry. He had never before walked so far, or felt so unhappy.

"It's very strange, but I feel exactly as if I had found my happy heart."

Just as the sun was setting the little prince came to a tiny house. It was very poor and weather-stained. It stood on the edge of the forest. But a bright light streamed from the window. So he lifted the latch, as a prince may, and went inside.

There was a mother rocking a baby to sleep. The father was reading a story out loud. The little daughter was setting the table for supper. A boy of the prince's own age was tending the fire. The mother's dress was old. There were to be only porridge and potatoes for supper. The fire was very small. But all the family were as happy as the little prince wanted to be. Such smiling faces and light feet the children had. How sweet the mother's voice was!

"Won't you have supper with us?" they begged. They did not seem to notice the prince's ugly frown.

"Where are your happy hearts?" he asked them.

"We don't know what you mean," the boy and the girl said.

"Why," the prince said, "to laugh and be as happy as you are, one has to wear a gold chain about one's neck. Where are yours?"

Oh, how the children laughed! "We don't need to wear gold hearts," they said. "We all love each other so much, and we play that this house is a castle and that we have turkey and ice cream for supper. After supper Mother will tell us stories. That is all we need to makc us happy."

"I will stay with you for supper," said the little prince.

So he had supper in the tiny house that was a castle. And he played that the porridge and potato were turkey and ice cream. He helped to wash the dishes, and then they all sat about the fire. They played that the small fire was a great one, and listened to fairy stories that the mother told. All at once the little prince began to smile. His laugh was just as merry as it used to be. His voice was again as sweet as music.

He had a very pleasant time, and then the boy walked part of the way home with him. When they were almost to the palace gates, the prince said: "It's very strange, but I feel just exactly as if I had found my happy heart."

The boy laughed. "Why, you have," he said. "Only now you are wearing it inside."

MY SON, THE TEACHER

Zig Ziglar

I love to play golf. As a matter of fact, there's almost nothing I enjoy more than just rarin' back and really bustin' that ball as hard as I can from the tee. (Then, if I can find it, I like to bust it again!) I don't play often because I discovered a long time ago that a fast game of golf and a slow game of golf both require approximately five hours. Since I average traveling nearly six thousand miles a week and am away from my family a large portion of the time, I have no desire to grab my sticks and head for the golf course on those occasions when I am home. But I do love to play golf.

So, about five years ago, I came up with a brilliant idea. I bought my redhead and my son, Tom, a set of golf clubs. Everybody was excited about it except my wife and son. They both decided to go along with me, however, and we started to play. After about five games my redhead said, "Honey, you know, I just don't like to play golf. It's either too cold or too hot, too wet or too dry, or too something, so count me out. I think you and Tom should go ahead and play because you need to spend some time privately with him." There went golf buddy number one.

At the end of the summer, my son said to me, "Dad, I really love to be with you, but I just don't like to play golf, so count me out." There went golf buddy number two and most of my golf for the next couple of years.

While returning from dinner one night two years later, we passed the driving range on North Central Expressway in Dallas. My sticks were in the back of the car and Tom said, "Dad, let's stop and hit a few."

Well, my son is a smooth talker, so we stopped to hit a few. After a while he said, "Dad, let me borrow one of your woods."

I protested and said, "Son, you are just too short. These woods are too long for you."

But Tom insisted, "Aw, Dad, just let me try one." So I handed him the four wood. He choked up on the club, leaned back, and busted that ball about forty yards further than I had ever seen him hit a golf ball before. The smile on his face was the second most beautiful smile I had ever seen on Tom, and I knew I had a golfing buddy.

The most beautiful smile appeared two days later at the country club. This club has two courses for golfers and another course for the real old folks and the real young folks. We played the other course. On one of the par fours Tom hit a beautiful wood shot right down the middle. Then he took his five iron and busted the ball onto the green about forty feet from the pin. Now he was hunting his bird.

To you nongolfers, that simply means that if he could sink this putt he would make that hole in one under par. I helped him line up and showed him about how hard to stroke the ball. He stroked it firmly and the ball went like it was tied to a string. BOOM! Right into the bottom of the cup. I'll tell you, the expression on that boy's face was the most beautiful thing I have ever seen. I grabbed him and hugged him and we did a war dance for about two minutes. He was almost as happy as I was.

Then I realized I had a problem. I was also on the green in two. I was about twelve feet from the cup hunting my bird. I feared if I missed my putt, Tom would figure I had missed it on purpose so he could win. This would have given him a cheap victory, which is a substantial loss. I wanted to give it my best effort, so if I missed I could honestly look at Tom and say, "Son, you won it fair and square."

Since my best effort always includes a little providential help, which is perfectly legitimate even on a golf course, I asked for that help on this particular hole and got it. I stroked the ball firmly and it, too, went straight to the bottom of the cup. Before I moved to pick up the ball, I looked Tom in the eye and said, "Now tell me the truth, Son. Were you pulling for Dad?"

Now I think you know what it would have meant to my boy had I missed the putt. He would have won his first hole of golf from his dad. It would have meant a lot to a twelve-year-old boy to win that first hole. But, without a moment's hesitation, quietly but firmly he said, "Dad, I always pull for you."

Without a moment's hesitation, quietly but firmly he said, "Dad, I always pull for you."

Now that's love. Pure love. That's what we need more of in every city, town, and village in America.

THE BIRTHDAY BALLOON

Sharla Taylor

Since my remarriage, my daughter, Melissa, had not accepted her stepfather's role of parent. There were many difficulties in the first few months. Melissa knew the boundaries and tried our patience regularly. She acted out at inappropriate times—usually in a public place to purposefully embarrass the two of us. My husband, Scott, was tired of his stepdaughter's precocious behavior and frustrated at the demands of becoming an instant father.

We had eaten at a local Italian restaurant for my daughter's ninth birthday. She had been extremely difficult that day. She took forever to decide what to eat, and then she didn't eat her entree, fought with her brother over dessert, and wouldn't leave the restaurant until she received her obligatory birthday balloon (in the exact choice as advertised in the newspaper flier). After the waiter dutifully returned with a pink latex balloon filled with helium and placed it in Melissa's hand, we left the restaurant and climbed into the car and headed toward home. The balloon was a floating hazard that blocked the rearview mirror. My husband sighed, parked on the side of the road, and carefully tied the balloon to the door handle on the passenger side of the car, where my daughter was sitting. Then we completed our journey home in silence. I could sense his growing frustration.

The thirty-eight-year-old bachelor I married was (and still is) an absolute "neat-nick," and he was having trouble adjusting to the clutter of two school-age children and a new wife moving into his home. His patience was frayed from the outburst at the restaurant, and he was anxious to get home and find a moment's solitude (which was an increasingly rare commodity in his heretofore peaceful bachelor's home).

When we pulled into the garage, Melissa carried her packages into the house and became distracted by playing with her gifts. Scott was irritated that, after she placed so much importance on getting a balloon of a particular color before we left the restaurant, Melissa hadn't even bothered to remove the balloon from the car and take it upstairs to her bedroom. Scott pulled his pocketknife from his trousers and opened the blade. He muttered angrily, "She just had to have it!" Scott stabbed the balloon with the blade of his knife, untied it from the handle of the car, crumpled the balloon into a knot, and threw it in the trash.

THE BIRTHDAY BALLOON

Melissa returned to the garage just in time to witness the murder of her birthday balloon. She froze in disbelief and horror, perceiving the death of the balloon to be a sinister act. Melissa was convinced that her stepfather was, indeed, a villain. She ran past me, shouting hysterically, "Mom, he popped my balloon! He popped my balloon!" Melissa raced upstairs, threw her body on the bed, and sobbed uncontrollably.

"How could you do that?" I scolded. He shrugged his shoulders and raised his hands in exasperation. My husband was guilty of reacting too quickly. In his attempt to clear out the car, he failed to realize that sometimes children need prompting to complete tasks, such as picking up after themselves. Annoyed, I trudged upstairs to calm my daughter. My husband left in the van. I presumed he "fled the scene" to settle his nerves. It had been a very trying day!

A few minutes later, I persuaded Melissa to come downstairs to the kitchen to have a glass of milk. When my husband returned home, he entered through the kitchen door, carrying a pink heart-shaped balloon that read, "Happy Birthday with Love." Scott knelt beside Melissa's chair and said, "I'm sorry." He presented the balloon to Melissa, whose tear-streaked face brightened with a surprised look. My husband continued his apology to Melissa. "I assumed you didn't want your balloon because you left it in the car. I am sorry that I broke something that was for you. You know, Melissa, you will have some disappointments in life along the way, but your mom and I will always be here for you. And although we may not always provide all things, we will always provide love; on that you can depend." Melissa threw her arms around Scott in a big bear hug.

It was the same big hug Melissa gave her stepdad when she graduated from high school. While cleaning her old room, I found the pink heart-shaped balloon folded and tucked in the corner of her keepsake drawer. I remembered that birthday and how much we had all grown as a family in the years that followed.

A dad's love never deflates, although his patience might!

A dad's love never deflates, although his patience might! Melissa's stepdad is readily available by telephone to talk her through how to change a flat tire when she drives back and forth to the university; and he is always there to lift her spirits when the rigors of college studies frustrate her. Their friendship has grown from antagonistic beginnings into one of mutual love, trust, and respect—and to think it all began with a burst balloon!

MOTHER'S DAY BREAKFAST

Patti Maguire Armstrong

It was an eventful Mother's Day when my young boys broke out of the mold of giving me presents orchestrated by their teachers. For many years I had received numerous little handprints dried into clay or pressed with paint onto paper, accompanied with the same old poem about this being a handprint that did not need to be wiped off. For the first time, they had planned something on their own.

As the day began, I could see through the slits in my bedroom blinds that a sparkling blue morning was underway. Accompanied by the early birds' breezy chirps, the house hummed of silence. With a husband, four boys eight and under, a dog, and a parakeet, it was a tune rarely played. I lightly tiptoed my way across the room, avoiding any floor-creaks that could wake a slumbering household. Once in the hall, I exhaled deeply, only moments away from a cup of warm tea and a spot of leisure with the newspaper.

CHAPTER THREE: *Hugs Show Love* . . .

When suddenly, what to my wondering ears did I hear, but a whispering child, blinking back a tear. "Mom," my oldest son, Aaron, called from the top of the stairs. "We were going to surprise you with breakfast in bed." His forlorn face looked down at me and asked, "What are you doing awake?"

"Me? Awake? No, no, I just thought I heard a noise. I'm going right back to bed."

So back to bed I went, this time taking no care to avoid the creaky floorboards. I lay on my back and stared at the ceiling's cobwebs that danced in a breeze emanating from my husband's rumbling snores. *Perhaps if I stuff Kleenex in Mark's mouth I could both silence and wake him*, I thought.

The Kleenex temptation became moot when the baby sounded his alarm. "Mamamamamamama," he called out. "Mark," I nudged, not quite gently. "Jacob is calling for you—and remember, it's Mother's Day." Mark obligingly rolled out of bed. "Happy Mother's Day," he mumbled, bobbing and swaying his way into the baby's room.

"And now that you are up, would you mind bringing me the newspaper?" I did not get an answer but moments later Luke, son number two, bounded in with several pages from the paper. "I think you dropped some of it," I commented, holding up a crumpled TV guide and the sports section.

MOTHER'S DAY BREAKFAST

He left to retrieve the rest, but his mind apparently wandered with his feet into the kitchen, which now was abuzz with small voices and clatter. By the time I had memorized the week's TV programming and the Minnesota Twins's batting averages, breakfast arrived with each boy carrying a plateful.

"We need to buy a serving tray next year," explained Tyler, son number three. "But don't worry," he assured me. "The food is great. We made it ourselves."

"Don't worry," he assured me. "The food is great. We made it ourselves."

I flashed a concerned look at my husband. "I was reading the paper," he explained. I manufactured a motherly smile for my three wide-eyed little fellows.

"Well, let's see, what do we have here? French toast, my favorite," I gushed, sampling a forkful. "Oh, it's crunchy."

"See, I told you that you couldn't get all the eggshells out using a towel," Aaron complained.

"Never mind," I said moving on to the next dish. "This cereal looks perfect, and the peanut butter toast is certainly thick and creamy. Wow, you must have scrambled a whole carton of eggs. Oh, boy, two bananas, and oh my, you boys certainly went to a lot of trouble to pick all the seeds out of this slice of watermelon. But what's this in my cup? There's not much in there."

"Tyler drank most of the chocolate milk he made you," Luke tattled.

"I did not," protested Tyler. "It spilled!"

"That's OK. Let's not worry about a little spilled milk," I comforted. "Well, I can see I'm going to need plenty of help eating this big, delicious breakfast," I said to my crowd of well-wishers.

"No thanks, I'm not hungry" . . . "Neither am I" . . . "Me neither," they responded. Mark waved the food away. "You know I never eat breakfast," he said in a panicked voice.

"We made it all just for you, Mommy," yelled Tyler.

"Mother's Day is sure fun," said Aaron.

"I'm having a great time," agreed Luke.

"Happy Mother's Day," said Mark.

"Thank you everyone," I smiled, "God has certainly blessed me." But then gazing upon my big Mother's Day feast, I was suddenly overcome with a new appreciation for all those little handprints I had received over the years. There were never leftovers to worry about.

LOVE'S POWER

Alan Loy McGinnis

During World War II, Victor Frankl was interned by the Germans for more than three years. He was moved from one concentration camp to another. He even survived several months at Auschwitz. Dr. Frankl said he learned early that one way to survive was to shave every day, no matter how sick you were, even if you had to use a piece of broken glass as a razor. For every morning, as the prisoners stood for review, the sickly ones who would not be able to work that day were sent to the gas chambers. If you were shaven, and your face looked ruddier for it, your chances of escaping death—at least for that day—were better.

Their bodies wasted away on the daily fare of 10½ ounces of bread and 1½ pints of thin gruel. They slept on bare board tiers seven feet wide, nine men to a tier. The nine men shared two blankets. Three shrill whistles awoke them for work at 3:00 A.M.

One morning as they marched out to lay railroad ties in the frozen ground miles from the camp, the accompanying guards kept

The truth—that love is the ultimate and the highest goal to which [we] . . . can aspire.

shouting and driving them with the butts of their rifles. Anyone with sore feet supported himself on his neighbor's arm. The man next to Frankl, hiding his mouth behind his upturned collar, whispered: "If our wives could see us now! I do hope they are better off in their camps and don't know what is happening to us."

Frankl writes:

That brought thoughts of my own wife to mind. And as we stumbled on for miles, slipping on icy spots, supporting each other time and again, dragging one another up and onward, nothing was said, but we both knew: each of us was thinking of his wife. Occasionally I looked at the sky, where the stars were fading and the pink light of the morning was beginning to spread behind a dark bank of clouds. But my mind clung to [that picture of my wife] . . . imagining it with an uncanny acuteness. I heard her answering me, saw her smile, her frank and encouraging look.

A thought transfixed me: for the first time in my life I saw the truth as it is set into song by so many poets, proclaimed as the final wisdom by so many thinkers. The truth—that love is the ultimate and the highest goal to which [we] . . . can aspire. Then I grasped the meaning of the greatest secret that human poetry and human thought and belief have to impart: . . . salvation is through love and in love.

It is perhaps the most powerful thought anyone can have. When we remember the primacy of love, and believe in our almost unlimited capacities for giving and receiving it, life can take on a vast joyfulness. Teilhard de Chardin once wrote: "Someday, after we have mastered the winds and the waves, the tides, and gravity, we will harness for God the energies of love, and then for the second time in the history of the world . . . [we] will have discovered fire."

CHAPTER FOUR

Hugs Whisper Prayers to the Heart

Prayer enlarges the heart

until it is capable of containing

God's gift of himself.

MOTHER TERESA

BEFORE YOU ASK

Helen Roseveare

One night I had worked hard to help a mother in the labor ward, but in spite of all we could do, she died, leaving us with a tiny premature baby and a crying two-year-old daughter. We would have difficulty keeping the baby alive as we had no incubator (since we had no electricity) and no special feeding facilities. Although we lived on the equator, nights were often chilly with treacherous drafts. One student midwife went to get the box we had for such babies and the cotton wool in which the baby would be wrapped.

Another student went to stoke up the fire and fill a hot-water bottle. She came back shortly in distress to tell me that as she filled the bottle it had burst. Rubber perishes easily in tropical climates. "And it is our last water bottle!" she exclaimed.

As in the West, it is no good crying over spilt milk, so in Central Africa it might be considered no good crying over burst water bottles. They do not grow on trees, and there are no drugstores down forest pathways.

"All right," I said. "Put the baby as near the fire as you safely can, and sleep between the baby and the door to keep it free from drafts. Your job is to keep the baby warm."

The following noon, as I did most days, I went to have prayers with the orphanage children. I gave the youngsters various suggestions of things to pray about and told them about the tiny baby. I explained our problem about keeping the baby warm enough, mentioning the hot-water bottle. The baby so easily could die if it got chills. I also told them of the two-year-old sister, crying because her mother had died.

Please, God, send us a water bottle. It'll be no good tomorrow, God, as the baby will be dead, so please send it this afternoon.

During the prayer time, one ten-year-old girl, Ruth, prayed the usual blunt prayer of our African children. "Please, God," she prayed, "send us a water bottle. It'll be no good tomorrow, God, as the baby will be dead, so please send it this afternoon."

While I gasped inwardly at the audacity of the prayer, she added by way of corollary, "And while you're about it, would you please send a dolly for the little girl so she'll know you really love her?"

As often with children's prayers, I was put on the spot. Could I honestly say, "Amen"? I just did not believe that God could do this. Oh, yes, I know that he can do everything. The Bible says so. But there are limits, aren't there? The only way God could answer this particular prayer would be by sending me a parcel from the homeland. I had been in Africa for almost four years and had never, ever received a parcel from home. Anyway, if anyone did send me a parcel, who would put in a hot-water bottle? I lived on the equator!

Halfway through the afternoon, while I was teaching in the nurses' training school, a message was sent that there was a car at my front door. By the time I reached home, the car had gone, but there, on the verandah, was a large, twenty-two-pound parcel. I felt tears pricking my eyes. I could not open the parcel alone, so I sent for the orphanage children.

Together we pulled off the string, carefully undoing each knot. We folded the paper, taking care not to tear it unduly. Excitement was mounting. Some thirty or forty pairs of eyes were focused on the large cardboard box.

From the top I lifted out brightly colored, knitted jerseys. Eyes sparkled as I gave them out. Then there were the knitted bandages for the leprosy patients, and the children looked a little bored. Then came a box of mixed raisins and sultanas that would make a nice batch of buns for the weekend. Then, as I put my hand in again, I felt the . . . could it really be? I grasped it and pulled it out. Yes, a brand-new, rubber hot-water bottle! I cried. I had not asked

God to send it; I had not truly believed that he could.

Ruth was in the front row of the children. She rushed forward, crying out, "If God has sent the bottle, he must have sent the dolly, too!" Rummaging down to the bottom of the box, she pulled out the small, beautifully dressed dolly. Her eyes shone! She had never doubted. Looking up at me, she asked, "Can I go over with you, Mummy, and give this dolly to that little girl so she'll know that God really loves her?"

The parcel had been on the way for five whole months! Packed up by former Sunday school class members whose leader had heard and obeyed God's prompting to send a hot-water bottle, even to the equator. And one of the girls had put in a dolly for an African child . . . five months before in answer to the believing prayer of a ten-year-old girl to bring it "this afternoon."

THE OWL AND THE PELICAN

Billy Graham

My wife has a weakness for books, especially old, choice religious books which are now out of print. At one time, Foyles' in London had a large secondhand religious book department.

One day during the 1954 London Crusade she was browsing through the books in Foyles' when a very agitated clerk popped out from behind the stacks and asked if she was Mrs. Graham. When she told him that she was, he began to tell her a story of confusion, despair, and frustration. His marriage was on the rocks, his home was breaking up, and business problems were mounting. He explained that he had explored every avenue for help and, as a last resort, planned to attend the services at Harringay Arena that night. Ruth assured him that she would pray for him, and she did. That was in 1954.

In 1955 we returned to London. Again my wife went into

Foyles's secondhand book department. This time the same clerk appeared from behind the stacks, his face wreathed in smiles. After expressing how happy he was to see her again, he explained that he had gone to Harringay that night in 1954 as he had said he would,

They were all now in the Lord's work—all because God spoke to him when he was "an owl of the desert"!

that he had found the Savior, and that the problems in his life had sorted themselves out.

Then he asked Ruth if she would be interested in knowing what verse it was that spoke to him. She was. Again he disappeared behind all the books and reappeared with a worn Bible in his hand. He turned to Psalm 102, which I had read the night that he had attended the Crusade. He pointed out verse 6, "I am like a pelican of the wilderness: I am like an owl of the desert" [KJV]. This had so perfectly described to him his condition that he realized for the first time how completely God understood and cared. As a result he was soundly converted to the Lord Jesus Christ. And subsequently so was his entire family.

My wife was in London during 1972 at the time of a Harringay reunion. As the ceremonies closed, a gentleman came up to speak to her, but he didn't have to introduce himself. She recognized the clerk from Foyles'. He was radiantly happy, introduced his

Christian family, and explained how they were all now in the Lord's work—all because God spoke to him when he was "an owl of the desert"!

How graciously God speaks to us in our need . . . often through some obscure passage.

T AND D

Vicki P. Graham

*I*n spite of her tiny size, she broke from her mother's womb fighting and fussing and, thankfully, perfect. Mona and Richard immediately named this long-awaited bundle of joy Tina, after Mona's mother, who had recently passed away. Naturally, it was no surprise that she was dubbed Tiny Tina almost from the start. Mona and Richard delighted in their bighearted and loving little girl. Her birth followed years of prayers for a baby, but they never dreamed they'd be blessed with such a beautiful and generous child.

When Tina was five, Mona and Richard put practicality aside and bought her a purebred golden retriever. The puppy's golden coat exactly matched Tina's own blond locks, and they made quite the pair as they fast became best friends. She named the puppy Sandy. It was hard for Tina to tear herself away from her buddy to start school that year, but resolutely she marched with her mom to the school bus to begin her school career. That afternoon, when Mona met the bus, Tina came bounding down the steps, face aglow.

"Mom, I got a new name," she yelled. "The kids like me. They gave me a new name. The kids said Tiny Tina is too hard to say, and we already have another Tina in class, so guess what my new name is?" Tina spilled out her excitement in one breath.

"My name is T. See, it stands for Tina. Isn't that cool?"

Breathing a sigh of relief, Mona told her child that T was a great name and, yes, she and Dad would also call her T. Mona was sure the nickname would fade away in the next few weeks.

The name stuck. By T's third year in school, no one but teachers even recalled her real name, Mona thought ruefully.

T and Sandy remained inseparable when she was out of school. The dog accompanied her, whenever possible, on visits to friends, outings, and trips to the store. It was for a simple errand to town that Richard decided to take along T and the pet. Mona blew kisses out the kitchen window at her little family, and they waved gaily as they drove away.

On the drive into town, a truck hauling concrete blocks blew a tire and swerved head-on into Richard's lane. There was nothing he could do, and he died instantly, the highway patrol officers assured Mona. They sadly informed her that the beautiful golden dog had been killed too. She slumped with relief, and with dread, when the troopers told her Tina had been badly injured and was on her way to the hospital. One of the men drove her car while she rode in the patrol car to the trauma unit.

For three hours Mona paced the surgery waiting room. Thankfully, friends had joined her by then, and they murmured words of encouragement and offered prayers for Tina. At last a doctor approached the little group.

"I have very good news," he smiled at Mona. "Your daughter should totally recover, except for one problem. Tina's ears were badly damaged. She will probably never hear again. She is totally deaf."

Mona collapsed into her friends' arms. She tried to focus on the good news, but all she could think was her precious T would never hear her mother's voice again, and how could she explain her daddy's and Sandy's deaths?

Somehow, Mona made it through the next few days. With her friends' help, she printed a letter to Tina about the car wreck. She could tell by Tina's expression that the eight-year-old comprehended that her faithful companion and her dad were dead. She didn't know if T's body-wracking sobs were for her loss or for the knowledge she'd never hear again.

When Tina finally arrived home from the hospital, she wandered the backyard morosely. She missed her doggy. At night she cried in loneliness when no warm, snuggly animal cuddled up next to her. When the doctors told Mona that she should try to enroll Tina in a school for the hearing impaired, Mona resisted. She knew she could handle any needs of Tina's, and she was determined not to remove her from the only school and town T had ever known.

Within weeks, however, and despite going back to school, Mona recognized the signs of depression in Tina.

"It's because she can't communicate to her friends or teachers without a lot of trouble," the school counselor told Mona. "She really needs to learn to sign, and so do you."

"But she can still talk," Mona protested, panicking at the very thought of sending her little girl away to school.

"Yes," the counselor patiently replied. "But in a few years people won't understand her as she loses her ability to correctly sound out words."

Mona knew the kind counselor was right, but she refused to entertain the idea of sending Tina away to school. She stubbornly researched for answers and finally found what she was looking for. A private academy for deaf children accepted day students who were not required to live on campus. The location was hundreds of miles from Mona's friends and relatives, but she resolved to make the move.

Mona thought her prayers were being answered when Tina seemed to regain her confidence at the new school. Unlike the first time, Mona was thrilled when her daughter came running in from school one day signing as fast as her little fingers would move.

"The school kids are calling me T, just like before," she spelled out. "Isn't that great? That means they like me."

"Wonderful," Mona signed back. She, along with other parents of hearing-impaired children, had learned to sign quite skillfully.

But something still wasn't healed for Tina. Mona couldn't understand what was responsible for the emptiness she saw in T's eyes, the lonely look that would pass over her little face when she thought her mom wasn't watching. The answer came suddenly one night when Mona glanced in the child's bedroom as she signed her nightly prayers.

"God, please send me another gold doggy," Tina prayed on her fingers, "one just exactly like my Sandy. Thank you."

She misses her dog! Mona realized. *I should have known that was the problem.*

Her thoughts were confirmed the very next day when Tina told her mom what she wanted for her birthday, which was coming up shortly.

"I want another golden retriever, Mommy," she said aloud. "Please, please, Mama."

Mona's heart broke, not just at the deterioration of Tina's speaking, but because her tight budget allowed no extra money for such an expensive purchase. Mona signed the standard adult answer for impossible requests from children: "We'll see." When

Tina's face fell and her eyes filled with tears, Mona resolved that she would find a way to fill the void for Tina.

Every day when she arrived home from work, Mona scanned the classified ads. She called every dog breeder in the telephone directory, and there were golden retrievers, all right, to the tune of six hundred dollars a puppy. Inquiries at pet stores turned up similar reports. Attempts to persuade Tina to accept another, less expensive breed of dog were fruitless. Tears would flow, and Tina would tell her mother that God was surely sending her exactly what she wanted for her birthday—another Sandy.

Do you suppose you could shed your grace on her another time and help us find the perfect dog, one that I can afford?

The day before Tina's celebration found Mona on her knees. "Father, you gave us Tiny Tina, and you allowed her to survive the wreck, and I'm so thankful. Do you suppose you could shed your grace on her another time and help us find the perfect dog, one that I can afford? Do your perfect will in our lives, Father. I trust you."

After Tina left for school on her birthday morning, Mona received a call from a church friend. The friend had found a dog breeder who had a litter of golden retrievers ready to leave their mother. She had no idea of the price but thought Mona might be able to talk him into her price range, if she went to see him personally.

Hope filled her heart as Mona made the drive to the breeder. Sure enough, the puppies were darling and exactly the color of Tina's beloved Sandy. Mona's hopes were crushed, however, when the owner told her these pups were the same as the going price, six hundred dollars. Mona explained that it was her little girl's birthday and she wanted more than anything to replace the dog that had been killed in the car wreck along with her husband. The man was sympathetic, he told her, but he must make money on these dogs, because it was his living.

Turning quickly so he wouldn't see the tears that threatened to overwhelm her, Mona walked away sadly.

"Wait a minute," he called after her. When she turned back, he walked to the fence and picked up a puppy that had gotten separated from his littermates.

"Lady, this is a pedigreed puppy, but I'll never be able to register him, and none of my customers will want to buy him for show purposes." He cradled the little ball of gold in his arms. "If you want him, you can have him."

Mona couldn't believe her ears. There must be something terribly wrong with the puppy if the breeder couldn't find anyone who wanted him.

"What's wrong that no one wants him?" she finally dared to ask.

"He's deaf," said the breeder. "Born deaf. Do you still want him?"

"Oh yes!" Mona said through her laughter and tears. "I want him. In fact," she said, cuddling the golden puppy, "he couldn't be more perfect."

As she started toward her car with the wiggly furball, she stopped. "By the way," she asked, "does the puppy have a name?"

The man grinned. "Well, it probably sounds silly, but he loves to dig, so we just call him D."

JUNIOR

Amy Hollingsworth

When you live in a town of one hundred people, it's usually not necessary to look out the window to check who's there before opening the front door (especially when, for most people in a small town, the front door is rarely used. Everyone knows to come in the back door, and knocking first is an optional courtesy). So when I heard the loud rap on the front door that morning, I didn't bother to look. Instead I swung open the door and caught sight of a tall, thin man I didn't recognize. He was dressed in mud-splattered coveralls with hair that looked like he had just awoken from a weeklong nap. His gaze was slightly vacuous. There was a splattering noise at his feet. If Jesus had asked me at that moment who my neighbor was, I would have pleaded, "Anyone but this man."

I stood frozen for a few seconds as I looked from the red-black puddle at his feet to the large cut of raw meat dripping blood through his fingers. He reached out his hands, and now the blood was dripping on the welcome mat that greeted visitors to the parsonage. "This is for you," he said, looking down and avoiding my widening eyes.

This was the first time I met Junior. My husband was pastoring a small rural church at the time, and we were enjoying the slow pace of the country in contrast to the bustle of the city we had just left. Usually when there was a knock at the door, it was someone with fresh vegetables from their garden, their "firstfruits" offering to the pastor. But this time it was Junior.

Junior was a bona fide hermit. Except for when he sold the vegetables from his garden to townsfolk or did piecemeal work for local farmers, he rarely had contact with people. A fiftyish bachelor who looked older than he was, Junior lived alone in a dilapidated house that slanted sideways and rested upon dirt floors. It was rumored that electricity and indoor plumbing were modern concoctions he could do without. Junior had worked as a farmhand for one of our deacons and had recently suffered a stroke. At the request of the deacon, my husband had gone to visit and pray with Junior in the hospital, and to show his appreciation, Junior had brought us a gift, venison in its most rudimentary state.

No matter how ill conceived Junior's show of appreciation was, he became my neighbor that day. He came to visit a second time, thankfully without a recently departed gift, and was standing in the living room, looking at an old painting I had just bought. I hadn't bothered to replace the cracked glass or refurbish the frame in any way; I liked it worn, still bearing the nicks and scuffs of time. My daughter, Emily, who was four at the time, watched Junior as he looked at the painting. Emily has always had an ethereal quality about her, as if she has a spiritual awareness of things most others aren't privy to and a deep compassion for anyone who is hurting. "My Mommy likes broken things," she said, her eyes moving from the painting to Junior, and then she added, "like you."

Junior *had* been broken by life, and like my distressed frame, no one had bothered to try to repair him. From what we could gather, his parents had either died or left him when he was a boy, and he had been raised by an uncle who had since died, leaving him completely alone. I wondered if my husband was the only visitor who came to see him in the hospital when he suffered a stroke. My husband had found him paging through a Gideon's Bible left in the hospital nightstand. Junior's sudden interest in his own mortality led to further conversation, and together my husband and Junior prayed for new life, eternal life.

A few months after our first meeting, we asked Junior to spend Christmas with us. When I greeted him at the door, the coveralls had been replaced by an old suit jacket, a few sizes too small, his long arms stretching beyond the jacket sleeves, which were ripped in the elbows. He had carefully smoothed down his hair. His wanting to dress up for our celebration deeply touched me; he was the most resplendent Christmas guest we'd ever had. He didn't eat much and left early after complaining of not feeling well, but his presence was the best part of the day for me. "Last night when I lay in bed," I wrote in my journal the next day, "I sensed the Lord giving us a gentle thank-you for min-istering to and feeding Him on Christmas Day. That was Jesus Himself in Junior's chair."

Madeleine L'Engle, in the second of her Time Quartet books, *A Wind in the Door*, issues a challenge to the young heroine, Meg Murry. The challenge comes through cherubim, represented in the single character Proginoskes (Progo for short), sent to enlist Meg's help in the cosmic battle between good and evil. Meg's task—her challenge—Progo tells her, is to be a "Namer."

" My mommy likes broken things," she said, her eyes moving from the painting to Junior, and then she added, "like you."

When Meg asks the angel what that means, he fumes, "I've *told* you. A Namer has to know who people are, and who they are meant to be."

"If someone knows who he is, really knows," the cherubim explains, "then he doesn't need to hate."[1] Feeling as good as possible about God's creation within us causes us to look upon our neighbor with the same sense of wonder and worth.

Then, once we are able to see the image of God in our neighbors, once we recognize their inherent value, we strive to help them become who they are meant to be. We "name" them.

We experienced this with our neighbor Junior. Having the grace to see the image of God in Junior allowed us to witness an even greater transformation: the image of God within him becoming conformed to the image of Christ.

After Junior prayed in the hospital with my husband for new life, he received it. On one of our visits to his home, he pulled my husband aside and told him that he knew a change had occurred in him because he was beginning to think differently. A fruit of that "thinking differently" was Junior's decision to go to neighbors with whom he had longstanding feuds and ask for forgiveness. He was looking through new eyes, eyes that recognized "what's wonderful" about his neighbor because they had recognized what was wonderful about himself. (This recognition of his self-worth even brought about some changes in his immediate environment, as he worked to cover up his dirt floors with cutout pieces of linoleum.)

My husband had talked to him about baptism, but Junior postponed the event because he hadn't been feeling well. But early on Easter morning he called Jeff and asked to be baptized that very day. When my husband asked about the change of heart and the immediacy of the request, Junior said he had been reading the book of Acts and had seen the directive to be baptized there.

JUNIOR

Our church family witnessed his rebirth: we became *his* family, perhaps the first real family he ever had. But the sickness he felt on Christmas Day had presaged what the new year would bring. His health began to deteriorate. The diagnosis, long delayed, of bone cancer finally arrived. He was returned to the same hospital where my husband had first met him.

The hospital was located forty-five minutes away, and I tried to visit Junior as often as I could. My last memory of him was trying to give him a kiss good-bye and missing as I tried in vain to pull myself over the bed rail. We both laughed. The next day, he didn't even remember I had been there. Then, late one Sunday night, Junior called my husband and asked him to spend the night with him at the hospital. He didn't want to be alone. Jeff was understandably exhausted after a full day of services at the church, but he went and spent the night with Junior.

"It's the last thing I'll ever ask of you, Pastor," Junior said. And it was. He died two days later, just three weeks after his initial diagnosis. In one year's time, my husband had prayed with Junior for new life, baptized him, and performed his funeral. We, his adopted family, watched that new life flourish into new thoughts and new healings in relationships, become sealed in baptism, and culminate in reunion with Christ. At Junior's funeral, a friend of his gave us his Bible, the one we had given him for Christmas, along with three photographs of Junior. Two were black-and-white pictures from his school days. One was of him as an adult. Perhaps they comprised the whole of Junior's family photo album.

In *A Wind in the Door*, Meg asks the cherubim how someone is Named, and the angel answers: "Love. That's what makes persons know who they are."[2]

A few weeks after Junior's death, I was back in Pittsburgh for my second interview with Fred Rogers ("Mr. Rogers"). I was waiting for him to complete some public-service announcements, so I was sitting out of the way toward the entrance to the studio. I can't remember the exact topic of the piece he was taping, but it had to do with an appeal to help others in need.

"I was thinking of Junior just then, as I said those words," Fred shouted to me from across the studio during a pause in taping.

"Is Junior your son?" a producer sitting near me asked, turning to look at me over her shoulder.

No, I thought to myself, *he's my neighbor.*

THE FAITH OF A CHILD

Jennifer Mihills

As we were frantically driving to Abilene, I kept thinking, *Could this be it? Are we finally going to be blessed with a child?*

The thoughts of this finally taking place were overwhelming and exiting. We had been praying for so long to have a child of our own. Years of infertility treatments and having one adoption fall through made us wonder if we would spend our lives without the joy of children. Every day we prayed and pleaded with God to bless us with a child. We thought it would never happen. Now, just minutes earlier, we had received a phone call from the birth mother. Her water broke and she was in labor at the hospital. She wanted us to hurry so that we could be in the delivery room to watch our little miracle being born.

Two and a half hours later, we finally arrived at the hospital. We waited, we paced, we stared at our watches. Finally it was time. Our child was born—our little gift from God we named Grace. God had answered our prayers.

For years we didn't understand His timing, but holding this precious little girl in our arms, we now knew why we needed to wait. God is faithful, God has listened, and God answered our prayers.

This blessing had made our lives so happy and so content we didn't think life could get any better. Then, twenty-three months later, it did. We had received a phone call about a birth mother who wanted us to be the parents of the child she was carrying. I was able to watch this new little miracle be born. God has blessed us once again with this little gift we named Nathan. God is faithful, God has listened, and God answered our prayers.

We feel so honored and blessed that we were chosen to be the parents of these two precious and beautiful children. As we raise them, we want them to know of God's love, His glory, His power, and His blessings. Our little girl, Grace, seems to know this so well. She understands it is God who has given her a house to live in. When she looks at her room, she knows God has blessed her with her toys. When she has a "boo-boo," she knows God will take care of it and heal it.

One day, she told me when she was a little baby she was inside my tummy. Although we have talked to her about her adoption before, I told her that Mommy's tummy was broken and was again talking to her about adoption. I thought she was listening as she stared at me intently.

She finally said, "Mommy, your tummy is broken? That's okay. I'll just pray to God and he will fix it."

Right then, Grace said her prayer, "Dear God, please, please, please fix my mommy's tummy. In Jesus's name, amen."

I thought that was the sweetest prayer. She was so concerned for her mommy. Three months went by and I became sick. At first I thought it was the flu, but the illness didn't go away. We were a little concerned and planned to make an appointment to see the doctor. When talking to a friend of mine, she suggested I take a pregnancy test.

Mommy, your tummy is broken? That's okay. I'll just pray to God and he will fix it.

"Why would I do that? I can't get pregnant!"

However, I decided to follow her advice and take a test before I called my doctor. How surprised and amazed I was when the test came back positive! *How can this be?* I showed my husband and there we stood, together in shock.

I went to the doctor and he confirmed that I was pregnant. That night, we sat at the kitchen table in disbelief and shock. After all these years, I was pregnant.

I told my husband, "I can't believe I have a baby in my tummy."

Grace overheard what I said, ran to me, and asked, "Did you say you have a baby in your tummy?"

I told her yes, and she jumped up and down yelling, "Yea, Mommy! God fixed your tummy! I knew He would fix it!"

Oh, the faith of a child! At such a young age she truly understands faith. If you ask Grace, "Why does your mommy have a baby in her tummy?" she will be very quick to answer, "Because I prayed for it."

Once again, God is blessing us. As I look at my children and feel the new life inside of me, I can't help but think, *God is faithful, God has listened, and God answered our prayers.*

Minor—Traveling Unattended

Jerry Seiden

*R*ight before the Jetway door closed, I scrambled aboard the plane going from L.A. to Chicago, lugging my laptop and overstuffed briefcase. It was the first leg of an important business trip a few weeks before Christmas, and I was running late. I had a ton of work to catch up on. Half wishing, half praying I muttered, "Please God, do me a favor, let there be an empty seat next to mine. I don't need any distractions."

I was on the aisle in a two-seat row. Across sat a businesswoman with her nose buried in a newspaper. No problem. But in the seat beside mine, next to the window, was a young boy wearing a big red tag around his neck: Minor—Traveling Unattended.

The kid sat perfectly still, hands in his lap, eyes straight ahead. He'd probably been told never to talk to strangers. "Good," I thought.

Then the flight attendant came by. "Michael, I have to sit down because we're about to take off," she said to the little boy. "This nice man will answer any of your questions, okay?"

Did I have a choice? I offered my hand, and Michael shook it twice, straight up and down.

"Hi, I'm Jerry," I said. "You must be about seven years old."

"I'll bet you don't have any kids," he responded.

I'm not afraid of dying. I'm not afraid because my mama's already in heaven.

"Why do you think that? Sure I do." I took out my wallet to show him pictures.

"Because I'm six."

"I was way off, huh?"

The captain's voice came over the speakers, "Flight attendants, prepare for takeoff."

Michael pulled his seat belt tighter and gripped the armrests as the jet engines roared. I leaned over, "Right about now, I usually say a prayer. I asked God to keep the plane safe and to send angels to protect us."

"Amen," he said, then added, "But I'm not afraid of dying. I'm not afraid because my mama's already in heaven."

"I'm sorry," I said.

"Why are you sorry?" he asked, peering out the window as the plane lifted off.

"I'm sorry you don't have your mama here."

My briefcase jostled at my feet, reminding me of all the work I needed to do.

"Look at those boats down there!" Michael said as the plane banked over the Pacific. "Where are they going?"

"Just going sailing, having a good time. And there's probably a fishing boat full of guys like you and me."

"Doing what?" he asked.

"Just fishing, maybe for bass or tuna. Does your dad ever take you fishing?"

"I don't have a dad," Michael sadly responded.

Only six years old and he didn't have a dad, and his mom had died, and here he was flying halfway across the country all by himself. The least I could do was make sure he had a good flight. With my foot I pushed my briefcase under my seat.

"Do they have a bathroom here?" he asked, squirming a little.

"Sure," I said. "Let me take you there."

I showed him how to work the Occupied sign and what buttons to push on the sink, then he closed the door. When he emerged, he wore a wet shirt and a huge smile.

"That sink shoots water everywhere!"

The attendants smiled.

Michael got the VIP treatment from the crew during snack time. I took out my laptop and tried to work on a talk I had to give, but my mind kept going to Michael. I couldn't stop looking at the crumpled grocery bag on the floor by his seat. He'd told me that everything he owned was in that bag. Poor kid.

While Michael was getting a tour of the cockpit, the flight attendant told me his grandmother would pick him up in Chicago. In the seat pocket a large manila envelope held all the paperwork regarding his custody. He came back explaining, "I got wings! I got cards! I got more peanuts. I saw the pilot, and he said I could come back anytime!" For a while he stared at the manila envelope.

"What are you thinking?" I asked Michael.

He didn't answer. He buried his face in his hands and started sobbing. It had been years since I'd heard a little one cry like that. My kids were grown—still I don't think they'd ever cried so hard. I rubbed his back and wondered where the flight attendant was.

"What's the matter, buddy?" I asked.

All I got were the muffled words, "I don't know my grandma. Mama didn't want her to come visit and see her sick. What if Grandma doesn't want me? Where will I go?"

"Michael, do you remember the Christmas story? Mary and Joseph and the baby Jesus? Remember how they came to Bethlehem just before Jesus was born? It was late and cold, and they didn't have anywhere to stay, no family, no hotels, not even hospitals where babies could be born. Well, God was watching out for them. He found them a place to stay: a stable with animals."

"Wait, wait," Michael tugged on my sleeve. "I know Jesus. I remember now." Then he closed his eyes, lifted his head and began to sing. His voice rang out with a strength that rocked his tiny frame. "Jeeesus looooves me—thiiiiis I knowwwwwww. For the Biiiiiible tells meeeeee sooooo . . ."

Passengers turned or stood up to see the little boy who made the large sound. Michael didn't notice his audience. With his eyes shut tight and voice lifted high, he was in a good place.

"You've got a great voice," I told him when he was done. "I've never heard anyone sing like that."

"Mama said God gave me good pipes just like my grandma's," he said. "My grandma loves to sing; she sings in her church choir."

"Well, I'll bet you can sing there too. The two of you will be running the choir." The seat-belt sign came on as we approached O'Hare. The flight attendant came by and said, "We just have a few minutes now." But she told Michael that it was important that he put his seat belt on. People started stirring in their seats, like the kids before the final school bell. By the time the seat-belt sign went off, passengers were rushing down the aisle. Michael and I stayed seated.

"Are you gonna stay with me?" he asked.

"I wouldn't miss it for the world, buddy!" I assured him.

Clutching his bag and the manila envelope in one hand, he grabbed my hand with the other. The two of us followed the flight attendant down the Jetway. All the noises of the airport seemed to fill the corridor.

Michael stopped. Slipping his hand from mine, he dropped to his knees. His mouth quivered. His eyes brimmed with tears.

"What's wrong, Michael? I'll carry you if you want."

He opened his mouth and moved his lips, but it was as if his words were stuck in his throat. When I knelt next to him, he grabbed my neck. I felt his warm, wet face as he whispered in my ear, "I want my mama!"

I tried to stand, but Michael squeezed my neck even harder. Then I heard a rattle of footsteps on the corridor's metal floor.

"Is that you, baby?"

I couldn't see the woman behind me, but I heard the warmth in her voice.

"Oh, baby," she cried. "Come here. Grandma loves you so much. I need a hug, baby. Let go of that nice man." She knelt beside Michael and me. Michael's grandma stroked his arm. I smelled a hint of orange blossoms.

"You've got folks waiting for you out there, Michael. Do you know that you've got aunts and uncles and cousins?"

She patted his skinny shoulders and started humming. Then

she lifted her head and sang. I wondered if the flight attendant told her what to sing, or maybe she just knew what was right. Her strong, clear voice filled the passageway, "Jesus loves me—this I know . . ."

Michael's gasps quieted. Still holding him, I rose, nodded "hello" to his grandma and watched her pick up the grocery bag. Right before we got to the doorway to the terminal, Michael loosened his grip around my neck and reached for his grandma.

As soon as she walked across the threshold with him, cheers erupted. From the size of the crowd, I figured family, friends, pastors, elders, deacons, choir members, and most of the neighbors had come to meet Michael. A tall man tugged on Michael's ear and pulled off the red sign around his neck. It no longer applied. As I made my way to the gate for my connecting flight, I barely noticed the weight of my overstuffed briefcase and laptop. I started to wonder who would be in the seat next to mine this time . . . and I smiled.

CHAPTER FIVE

Hugs Bring Hope to the Heart

The capacity to care gives life its

deepest significance.

PABLO CASALS

CRAB APPLE TREE

Cathy Lee Phillips

"Meet me at the tree!"

Residents of Posey Road uttered this phrase often during my childhood. Though countless trees populated the property, everyone knew exactly which tree we meant.

Situated in a small pasture near the house, the crab apple tree was part of the history and heritage of our farm. As a shade tree, it was terrific; as a climbing tree, it was exceptional. Young Posey Road residents congregated there regularly to play freeze tag (you were "safe" as long as you touched the tree), hide and seek, and an infinite number of games we invented. That tree witnessed many ferocious softball games while faithfully serving as second base. I spent many quiet summer afternoons beneath that tree— dreaming, reading, and writing while snacking on Oreos and a thermos of cherry Kool-Aid.

The tree was an old friend, one I especially loved in the springtime. Even now I can close my eyes and picture its delicate pink-white flowers. I can smell the pleasing fragrance of its abundant blossoms. That sweet perfume often traveled on the night breeze and tiptoed into my bedroom through the open window. I fell asleep to the familiar song of the whippoorwill and the pleasing fragrance of the crab apple blossoms.

Several years ago, I developed a hankering for a crab apple tree of my own. I shared my Posey Road memory with my husband, Jerry. I wanted a crab apple tree to bud and blossom in our own yard each spring.

"I hereby decree that on Saturday we will travel unto Pike's nursery and purchase a flowering crab apple tree!" I declared. Smiling, Jerry turned back to whatever book he was reading at the time.

But he listened. On Saturday morning I prepared for "Operation Crab Apple." I arose early and cooked breakfast (translation: I actually heated our Pop-Tarts!). I gassed up Jerry's revoltingly ugly blue truck. I located shovels and rakes. But as I rushed, I noticed a definite lack of enthusiasm on his part.

"What's the problem? I decreed that we would purchase a crab apple tree today. Get moving . . . the clock is ticking!"

Jerry smiled and calmly asked, "Cathy, have you been outside?"

"Of course I've been outside," I retorted. "Haven't you seen me running around all morning? Get it in gear, Jer."

"But, Cathy, have you paid attention to what is outside?"

Paid attention to what was outside? Was he losing his mind? There were a million things outside. What was I to pay attention to?

"Just slow down," he instructed softly as he guided me toward the front door. "Now look to your left."

And there it was—a flowering crab apple tree planted smack in the middle of the front yard of our Henderson Mill Road home. I stared in amazement.

"I bought and planted that tree three days ago," Jerry related. "You've rushed by it for three days but have been too busy to notice. Slow down, Cathy. Don't miss the good things all around you."

Yes, I felt about three inches tall . . . only slightly shorter than I actually am. So I stopped, opened the curtains, and gazed at that little tree through tear-filled eyes. The world rushed on,

I savored the love that showed itself in the tender hands that planted a tiny crab apple tree just outside our front door.

but I stopped and wrapped myself in my husband's arms. I savored the love that showed itself in the strong arms that held me, the gentle words that taught me, and the tender hands that planted a tiny crab apple tree just outside our front door. I am grateful for that day—we created memories that would sustain me following my husband's death only months later.

Years after Jerry died, I sold the house on Henderson Mill

Road. As the real estate agent completed her paperwork, she asked if there were any special stipulations for the sales contract.

"Just one," I replied. Pointing to the crab apple tree, I advised her, "This tree leaves with me."

"You are taking a tree with you?" she asked incredulously.

"Absolutely."

So it was written. So it was done.

My friends Gene and Mike uprooted the tree and replanted it in my new yard in South Carolina. And when I moved back to Georgia in 1999, Mike and Gene returned—holding shovels and their aching backs.

"You are the only person we know to travel with her own crab apple tree," they chuckled. But, in love, they uprooted the tree and transplanted it in the yard of my new home in Georgia.

Well, spring has come and my crab apple tree is budding. I love that tree and the memories it evokes—childhood games of tag and softball, quiet dreams of what life would hold, and the precious gift of a husband's unconditional love, a love that survives even the separation of death. In faith I watch my crab apple tree awaken to bud and blossom, and in amazement I witness the promise of hope and resurrection in each precious flower.

THE TEACHER'S CHALLENGE

India M. Allmon

As a new teacher entering my sixth-grade classroom, I was soon greeted by those teachers who had preceded me with those same students. They gave me a very vivid description of what lay ahead for me. For the past five years, each in turn had tried every known method to deal with an incorrigible boy whom I shall call Will. To cope with his behavior, teachers had deprived him of playground privileges, paddled him, sent him to the office, and expelled him. Others tried granting him special privileges such as allowing him to be one of the captains in choosing players for the spelling match or the ball team—anything to build self-esteem. My friends warned me that all their efforts had been in vain.

By my third day I realized that my teacher friends had not exaggerated. In the classroom he repeatedly yelled out as I talked; he tripped anyone who walked down the aisle. Often he would lie on the floor or throw erasers across the room and even become profane at times.

I had no success in dealing with him in the presence of his peers, so ours turned out to be a one-on-one affair. In these sessions he was always in a sullen pout, sometimes refusing to answer me, other times yelling at me. Little by little I sensed a bit of devotion to his mother. Also I noted that he was very proud of his pet rooster, Sambo. When my patience was almost exhausted, I reasoned that we all have a weak, vulnerable spot somewhere. It was then that I resolved to find Will's Achilles' heel. Finally, I inquired if I might visit his mother and likewise get to see Sambo. His consent was slow in coming, but finally he did agree.

When my patience was almost exhausted, I reasoned that we all have a weak, vulnerable spot somewhere.

Before my visit I learned that his irresponsible father was a truck driver who seldom came home, and neither did his paycheck. The mother was terminally ill with tuberculosis, and the fifteen-year-old daughter had dropped out of school to care for the mother.

When I arrived at Will's home, I found a very dilapidated house with meager furnishings. In the absence of chairs I even sat on an apple crate. The poor, bedridden mother was very weak yet thanked me for coming. Next I got to see Sambo. Will had trained him to crow so that he might be rewarded with a few grains of corn. Also he would stand on tiptoe, then fly upward to get a morsel of bread that Will held high above his head.

Although Will was somewhat sociable when I visited his home, the old sullen, obstinate attitude was still very prevalent in the classroom. In privacy I often inquired about his mother or asked if Sambo had learned any more tricks. My visits continued, and I took food and various articles to add to the mother's comfort. I even took seeds and a leg band for Sambo. I noticed a wee bit of improvement.

When school resumed following our Thanksgiving holidays, Will was at his worst, obnoxious to his classmates and completely ignoring me. At the close of that unbearable day when the children were going home, I plucked Will's sleeve and asked him to remain with me for a few minutes. Alone, I asked why he was so ugly today. I got no reply; instead he just stared, acting as if he could neither hear nor speak. Finally, when I noticed that he was trembling, I laid my arm across his shoulders as he blurted out, "They killed Sambo so that we could have something to eat for Thanksgiving dinner."

The two of us sat on a bench side by side for a long time, my arm around his shoulders, with tears running down both our cheeks. Friends in loss. Friends at last.

REMEMBER THE FRANDSENS

Kathryn Forbes

The summer that I was twelve, I vacationed at my uncle's ranch in Santa Clara Valley, California. I was a reluctant visitor. That is, until I met Smithy.

Smithy, who lived on the next ranch, was the most forthright and the most completely adult boy I'd ever known. My aunt said it was because Smithy's parents died before he was eight, and a bachelor uncle had had to rear the boy as best he could. My uncle said that hardworking farm boys were usually old for their years, even at twelve.

Becoming friends with Smithy wasn't easy. I soon learned that the slightest lapse into things either fanciful or childish sent Smithy scurrying. He had an annoying habit of disappearing whenever he got bored or discomfited. My aunt said his real name was Lloyd, but he never admitted it; one called him Smithy, or went unanswered.

Remember the Frandsens

When the old Horlick farm was sold, by mail, to an Eastern couple named Frandsen, I thought it exciting because I had heard that the new owners were stage people. Smithy remained non-committal, but on the day I chose to happen to walk up the Frandsens' driveway, Smithy was with me. And when, halfway up the walk, we bumped right into Mr. and Mrs. Frandsen and they greeted us with exclamations of joy and welcome, Smithy was too surprised to run away.

The newcomers were, I judged, nearly fifty. Mrs. Frandsen had a beautiful, soft face, and her lovely blond hair was just touched with gray. Mr. Frandsen was shorter than his wife, although he held himself exceedingly straight, and his little brown eyes twinkled with kindness.

We were their very first visitors, they said; we must come out of the hot sun and into the cool of the house. Neither Smithy nor I had ever met grownups like this before. We were not used to sitting in front rooms decorated with spears and masks and signed photographs of costumed ladies and gentlemen, nor to being served tea out of something called a samovar.

Most of all, we were not used to being treated as happy contemporaries. The Frandsens told us exciting anecdotes about New York, about their experiences when they had acted in road companies. We were allowed to glimpse their future plans, the dreams-that-were-going-to-come-true, now that they had retired and settled down.

George—of course we were to call them George and Lisa, were we not their first new friends?—was going to become a real farmer. He had all the Government bulletins. Most wonderful of all, the Frandsens were going to adopt a baby. "A baby girl," Lisa said, "with blue eyes."

George beamed. "For months, now, we have had our request in. When we came through San Francisco we filled out final forms."

"And always," Lisa said, "we'll tell her that we chose her." They showed us the books they had about raising babies. Now, as soon as the Agency people sent a lady down to inspect them, the baby would be theirs.

I couldn't stay away from the Frandsens. They enchanted me.

Smithy and I stayed on and on. Never had I felt so welcome, such a distinguished guest. I chattered, and no one said it was time for me to go home, or that my mother wanted me. When Lisa tried to get Smithy to talk, too, and asked his name, I—drunk with social success—blurted out that it was Lloyd Smith. Lisa said Lloyd was a fine name. I expected something to happen, but Smithy just rolled his eyes alarmingly, and looked, for a moment, like my uncle's colt.

When we finally stood up to go, George and Lisa said we were to come back often, and Lisa kissed my cheek.

I couldn't stay away from the Frandsens. They enchanted me. They called their stove Ophelia, because it was quite, quite mad.

REMEMBER THE FRANDSENS

They named their bantam rooster Iago; their pig was Falstaff. When we sat on the cool side porch, George and Lisa told me whole plots out of plays, even acted them out. Sometimes I would catch a glimpse of Smithy, out in the orchard, and he would be listening too.

When my uncle's farm dog, Old Ben, died of age, and no one but me was sad about it, I lugged the poor hound's body over to the Frandsens'. Halfway there, Smithy materialized, and took over my burden. He helped George dig a grave of honor at the foot of the Frandsens' pepper tree. After it was over, Smithy listened quietly while George said the most beautiful words I had ever heard: "Fear no more the heat of the sun, or the furious winter's rages . . ."

As the days went on I despaired of making Lisa understand that Smithy was not a child. When she baked bread she sent him miniature loaves; when she made cake there was always a tiny one, baked in the lid of the baking powder tin, for Smithy. Obediently, I delivered them; silently, he pocketed them.

On the Saturday that the Agency lady came to inspect the Frandsens I went into the orchard, to be out of the way. I found Smithy there. We each picked a tree, leaned against it, and settled down to wait. I wasn't worried; anyone could see that the Frandsens were remarkable people.

"And the way they do everything," I said, "with—well, with ceremony. Smithy, aren't they wonderful?"

Smithy just grunted. I noticed, though, when we heard the Agency lady's car clatter away that he was on his feet as quickly as I. The moment we entered the house, we knew that something was terribly wrong.

Lisa was sitting quietly in a chair. She didn't look gay or young anymore. George patted her shoulder, while he told us.

"We are too old. People past forty-five are not permitted to adopt small babies."

I was indignant. "But they must have known—the forms—"

George looked down. "In the theater, one takes off a year here, a year there. Truly, Lisa and I had forgotten—" He shrugged. "Today we told our true ages. The Agency lady is kind, but it is a new rule."

"I can understand," Lisa said bravely. "It is for the child's good. So that—so that a child shall not have old—parents." She began to cry.

I was suddenly aware of being a child, too, without experience or knowledge. I did not know what to say to my friends, how to comfort them. And Smithy was no help. He slipped away without a word.

When, a little later, we heard a thump on the porch, I had a wild hope that it might be the Agency lady coming back. But it was only Smithy. He had his Sunday suit on, and the knickers were too short, and he looked funny. He gave me a terrible frown, and set down three newspaper-wrapped packages and two fishing poles. Standing there in the open doorway, he said matter-of-factly, "People are always adopting children; why can't it be the other way around once in a while?" His voice began to climb. "So I choose you. I asked my uncle, and he doesn't care, because he wants to move to the city anyway. So if you—if you want—"

Lisa ran across the room and put her wet cheek against Smithy's face, and said, "Lloyd! Oh, Lloyd!" I was afraid she was going to try to kiss him, and I wished somebody would shut the door. I guess George understood, because he started shaking Smithy's hand manfully, and saying, "Well, now, welcome, welcome."

Smithy seemed to make some tremendous effort. "Isn't there some sort of ceremony?" he asked George. "Shouldn't you—carry me into the house, or something?"

"But that's a ceremony for—" I started to say, but couldn't finish.

I do not think that twelve-year-old girls are particularly aware of poignancy, but I do know that the scene, that day, touched me beyond tears. Vainly trying to swallow the hurting in my throat, I watched George Frandsen stoop and lift the tall, gangly boy, the long, black-stockinged legs awkwardly disposed. Gently, carefully, he carried Smithy over the threshold and into the house.

"Well, now," I heard George say, "well, now, Son . . ."

TWICE BLESSED

Nancy Eckerson

My little girl, Jamie, and I sat upstairs in her bedroom, basking in the sunlight, one spring morning. I was combing her long, blond-streaked, red hair as we were getting ready to leave for church.

As I ran the brush from her crown down to her shoulders, I was awed by the golden glow intertwined with the deep red and auburn hair that cascaded down her little back. Fascinated, I stroked her hair and watched as her natural shine and the illuminating rays of sunlight played together to form an iridescent twirl of vibrant colors.

Slowly, as I brushed again and again, my mind trailed off to memories of the beautiful amber, deep browns, and the rusty reds of those long-ago molasses taffy pulls in my grandmother's kitchen. It was at that moment that the story of my special blessing with Grandma came alive.

TWICE BLESSED

My grandmother was a beautiful woman. Her silvery-white hair was always done up in a fashionable style. She wore a touch of pinkish rouge on her cheeks, just enough to make her look vibrantly healthy. She was always dressed to the nines. Her outfits were adorned with stunning brooches complimented by matching earrings and necklaces.

I can see her now in her deep raspberry-pink knit ensemble, with the white trim on the sleeves and collar. She wore large pearl earrings to set off the little pearl buttons that ran down the front of the sweater. As always, her lipstick matched her clothes, and her shoes and handbag always matched her lipstick.

I loved my grandmother. From the time I can remember, she would allow me to go upstairs to her bedroom and explore her dressing-table fare. She had row after row of exquisite bottles of sweet perfume. Among my favorites were the crystal hourglasses, the tall crackle-glass bottles, and the tiny cut-glass triangle with a black-faced bottle topper with wild black hair. I remember telling her that I imagined she must have gone to Africa and gotten that one on a safari. She didn't say yes, but she didn't say no. She just indulged my love of fantasy and let me make up story after story.

The glassy surface of the dressing table was topped with a white linen scarf. A golden, mirror-lined tray on the table held Grandma's expensive vanity set. I admired the brush, made of finest horsehair, mounted on a golden frame; the fine-toothed comb lined with gold; and the handheld "looking glass" trimmed with ornate gold. Grandma's initials were engraved on the brush and the looking glass. I felt so grown-up and regal just touching them.

Grandma's dresser boxes were another special treat that added great mystique to my initiation into this feminine world. I would dab the puff from her powder box and proceed to powder my nose. My clumsy young hands, not so adept at fine motor skills, made my dabs more like pounces. Developing the fine art of nose powdering rendered a cloud of dust that turned my face and Grandma's table white with powder. And still she smiled.

Grandma was known throughout our town for her smile. It lit up her face and the faces of those around her. Her eyes would even join in the joy, and you could tell she was smiling even if you could only see her forehead and eyebrows. When she was happy, my grandfather smiled too. He always looked so proud to walk with Grandma on his arm. They were very much in style and equally as much in love.

She made sure that we Eckerson cousins got together. Sometimes we would play together while she cooked up her special hard chocolate sauce for ice cream sundaes. It was the sweetest kind of chocolate that cracked when you dug your spoon into it. Sometimes she would have Easter egg hunts for us, and you could hear her whisper secret hiding spots to the little ones so no one felt left out.

But my all-time best memory with my grandma was the annual taffy pull. She made the best molasses taffy, and we kids were employed to do the pulling that made it soft and chewy. With one cousin on each end, we'd pull and pull, then wrap the taffy, doubled back on itself, twisting it like a braid, then we'd pull and pull again. This process was repeated over and over.

Pulling taffy would create an earth-toned rainbow. The longer the stretch, the blonder the sweet confection would appear.

Grandma would know just when the time was right, and we would set the glob of taffy on the table. She would then snip off bite-sized pieces, and we would wrap them in waxed paper, twisting the ends closed.

The goodies were divvied up, and each of us would be given a bag of fresh molasses taffy to take home with us. I loved my little cousins and found great joy in getting to know them during these taffy pulls. I would leave, feeling that my family was the very best in town. And I would always leave with the thought that Grandma was part of the reason why.

My family was the very best in town. And I would always leave with the thought that Grandma was part of the reason why.

So you can imagine my puzzlement when the townsfolk would say, "Your grandma would be so proud of you," after I would finish a solo at church or sing in the school musical. Confused, I would frown and say, "My grandma is proud of me. She is right here with me." Folks would simply nod and give me one of those knowing looks.

By the time I was twelve, the picture became clearer. Grandma Alberta was not my "real" grandma. Peg was the name I kept hearing over and over again. It was Peg to whom people were referring when they said my grandma would be so proud.

I finally asked my mother to explain. She told me of the death of my natural grandmother before I was born. It was such a tragedy that people didn't speak much about it, for fear of upsetting my grandfather. Grandma Peg was only in her late forties when her heart, already weakened from childhood rheumatic fever, gave out. She left behind three children.

I summoned up the courage to ask my dad to talk about his mom. As he reminisced, it was very plain for me to see that Dad adored his mother. The stories of her antics and her sense of humor enthralled me, hour after hour. He boasted of her musical awards and the people she helped with their musical careers. He showed me sheet music of love songs that Grandma Peg had written for Grandpa. They had been very much in love.

The amazing part was that, like me, Peg was a dedicated musician. My musical talent was my link to my precious grandmother. As these revelations sunk in, I nearly burst with joy. Not only did I have a talented and beautiful Grandma Peg, who lived in heaven, but I had a kind and beautiful Grandma Alberta who lived on earth, as well.

As I finished brushing Jamie's molasses taffy-colored hair, I came to another realization. Not only had my grandfather married his high-school sweetheart and had three beautiful children, but after the agony of losing his first love, God had given him a second blessing. He was to spend the rest of his days with another very special woman. He had been twice blessed.

Party in Room 210

Tony Campolo

I head up an organization that has created a missionary enterprise in Haiti. Presently, through the efforts of those who have taken over this ministry, a network of some eighty-five schools has been established that serves children who have been reduced to a life that is pretty close to slavery. The children in these schools, for the most part, come from families that are so poor they have had to give their children away to other families who can feed them. These oppressed youngsters are given the most menial tasks imaginable, and they can expect to spend their lives in hard labor. Such children carry water for most of the day and, in between, work in the sugar fields. Classes are held from the late afternoon into the evening because these children are not free to go to school during the regular daytime hours. Nevertheless, they attend the school with great faithfulness, because they know that if they can learn to read and write, in a country where the illiteracy rate is 85 percent, they have a chance to escape their oppressive lives.

When I go down there I usually stay at a Holiday Inn right in the center of Port-au-Prince. Once, when I was walking to the entrance of the hotel, I was intercepted by three girls. I call them girls because they looked to be about fifteen or sixteen years of age. The one in the middle said, "Mister, for ten dollars you can have me all night long." I was stunned by what she had said. I turned to the girl next to her and asked, "Can I have you for ten dollars?" She nodded approval.

"Mister, for ten dollars you can have me all night long."

I asked the third girl the same question. She tried to conceal her contempt for me with a smile. But it's hard to look sexy when you're fifteen or sixteen and you're very poor and your family is hungry.

I said, "Fine! I've got thirty dollars! I'm in Room 210. You be up there in a half hour. I'll pay you then and I want all three of you for the whole night!"

I rushed up to the room and got on the phone, and called down to the concierge desk. I said, "Send every Walt Disney cartoon video you have up to Room 210. Anything by Disney. Send it up to me."

I called down to the restaurant and asked if they made banana splits. I told them that I wanted banana splits with

145

extra everything. I wanted them to be huge and delicious. I wanted extra whipped cream, extra chocolate syrup, extra nuts. I wanted . . . I wanted . . . four of them!

Within the half hour the videos came, the three girls came, and the banana splits came. I sat the girls down on the edge of the bed. We ate the banana splits. We watched the videos. We had a little party as we watched the videos until about one in the morning. That's when the last of them fell asleep across the bed.

As I sat there in the stuffed chair looking at their little bodies strewn across the bed, I thought to myself, *Nothing's changed! Nothing's changed! Tomorrow they will be back on the streets. Tomorrow they will be selling their little bodies for ten dollars a throw, because there will always be rotten ugly men who will destroy the dignity of little girls for ten dollars a night. Nothing's changed!*

Then the Spirit spoke to me and said, "But, for one night, Tony, you let them be little girls again. For one night, you let them be kids. You didn't change their lives, but for one night you gave them back their childhoods." I am convinced that that little expression of love and that little party in Room 210 of the Holiday Inn in Port-au-Prince was the work of the Holy Spirit.

A LITTLE GLIMPSE OF HEAVEN

Chuck Terrill

*H*eaven is a little hard to understand. Sometimes we do catch a glimpse of it. We may not be looking for it particularly, it just flashes through. I caught a little glimpse of heaven, once.

A gray-haired lady was struggling with several bags in the Knoxville Airport. It wasn't until after I asked her if I could help her that I noticed the infant she carried.

"That's a cute baby. How old is she?" I asked.

"Just three days." The lady smiled.

I carried her things on board and stowed them while she got settled. My seat was two rows back, across the aisle. I watched the lady and the baby and thought the scene a little odd. She was fiftyish, the baby an infant. An airplane flight. It didn't make sense.

I had to change planes in Memphis, and apparently the lady

147

did too. I asked to help with her bags again. She thanked me.

"Your baby is still sleeping."

"Oh, it's not my baby. I'm just delivering her," she explained as I followed her toward the exit.

When we stepped from the DC-10 into the waiting area of gate eleven, I slowly began to understand.

Her life was forever, irrevocably changed. What grace, what boundless love.

A frazzled young couple waited. The husband appeared to be physically supporting his trembling wife. Her eyes were filled with tears. Her lips trembled.

Then she saw the baby.

She stripped the baby down to its diaper. With wide eyes she turned the infant this way and that, examining her like a jeweler would a fine diamond. Then she clutched that child to her chest and sat on the floor and wept.

Through the tears she asked the lady about the baby's mother. I listened in, mesmerized.

"She's OK," the social worker said. "She spent this morning with the baby in her hospital room. We took some pictures. She said good-bye, then we caught our plane."

This was a little glimpse of heaven! An infant girl closed

her eyes in Knoxville and woke up in Memphis in the arms of someone *else* who loved her. Her life was forever, irrevocably changed. What grace, what boundless love.

The couple with their new baby walked out of the airport into a new life.

"My plane returns in an hour."

It was the gray-haired lady. I was still holding her bag.

"Oh," I said as I handed it over. I nodded to the departing couple. "Does that happen often?"

She sighed.

"Not enough. But when it does, it's worth everything."

"Everything," I thought as I watched the trio pass out of sight. "Just like heaven."

CHAPTER SIX

*Hugs Make Music
in the Heart*

Of all the music that reached

farthest into heaven, it is the

beating of a loving heart.

HENRY WARD BEECHER

THE GIFT OF CARING

Arthur Gordon

Years ago, with two other college students, I was traveling one spring vacation in Spain. In Malaga we stayed in a pensión that was comfortable enough but strangely somber. The owner, who spoke English, had little to say. His wife, a tall, tragic-looking woman, always wore black and never smiled. In the living room an enormous grand piano stood silent. The little Spanish maid told us that the Señora had been a concert pianist, but that two years ago her only child had died. She hadn't touched the piano since.

One afternoon we three American youngsters visited a *bodega*, a wine cellar where sherry was stored. The affable proprietor urged us to sample various vintages, which we were not at all reluctant to do, and we sang and danced all the way home. Back at the house, full of thoughtless gaiety, one of my friends sat down at the great piano, flung back the dusty keyboard cover, and began to play, very badly, while we supported him at the top of our lungs.

CHAPTER SIX: *Hugs Make Music . . .*

Suddenly the maid rushed into the room, looking appalled. Behind her came the owner, hands outstretched in a pleading gesture. "No, no," he cried. "You mustn't!" At the same instant another door opened, and there stood the Señora herself, dark, tragic eyes fixed on us. The music died. For an endless moment, all of us were frozen with dismay and embarrassment.

The Señora kept playing, magnificent, soaring music that filled the whole house, driving the grief and the shadows away.

Then suddenly this woman saw how miserable we were. She smiled, and great warmth and beauty came into her face. She walked forward, pushed my friend aside, sat down and began to play.

I remember how the maid hid her face in her hands, how the husband looked as if he wanted to burst into tears. The Señora kept playing, magnificent, soaring music that filled the whole house, driving the grief and the shadows away. And young though I was, I knew that she was free—free because she had felt pity for us, and the warmth of compassion had melted the ice around her heart.

MUSIC LESSONS

Katherine Grace Bond

Nobody asked if I wanted a "junior-high buddy." I just got called to the office, where I practically lived anyway.

Anything that went wrong at Orville Wright Elementary—the fifteen pairs of underwear up the flagpole, the urinal that played "Jingle Bells" whenever someone flushed—whatever it was, I got blamed.

Sitting in Mrs. Kellerman's office was a kid, older than me and with skinny brown arms. He grinned real fast when I came in.

"Kyle, this is Austin Atterberry." Mrs. Kellerman stuck a fat file—mine—back in the cabinet. "Austin is an eighth grader at Edison. He's agreed to be your junior-high buddy."

So when did I agree to it? I thought. The kid stood up. He was tall, real tall.

"I bet you play basketball," I said.

"Nope," he said. "Piano."

It's not like I needed looking after. My parents worked and the kids in my neighborhood already had friends, so I was used to being on my own. But every afternoon Austin was by my locker sucking on a sourball. It wasn't bad, I guess. With Austin around, no one beat me up.

He was right when he said he didn't play basketball. His throws always hit the rim. I beat him every time.

"If you're going to be a man, little bro, you gotta turn the other cheek."

Austin shook his head when I showed how I'd wired our doorbell to open the neighbor's garage, but he had great ideas for my railroad.

The only thing that bugged Austin about my house was that there was no piano.

"Here she is." Austin ran his hands over a Yamaha PR-500 keyboard. We were at Harmony Music. "Mrs. Goodwin says if a piano won't fit in the apartment, this is the next best thing."

Mrs. Goodwin taught Austin piano. He washed her windows for it, even though she said he didn't have to. If someone gave me a freebie, I wouldn't pay for it.

"I've made six months of payments," he said. "Only a hundred dollars to go."

"How'd you get all that money?"

"Oh, mowing lawns, baby-sitting."

"Baby-sitting. What does my dad pay to keep me busy?"

Austin turned sharply. "No one pays me. I do this because I want to."

I didn't believe him. "Well, play something," I said.

When Austin turned on the power, a scowling clerk bustled over. "Do you need help, boys?" he asked. "These are sensitive instruments—for musicians."

"How do you know we're not musicians?" I imitated his snobby voice. "For your information, Austin practically owns—"

"Chill, Kyle," Austin cut in. "The man's new; the manager knows me."

He nodded and stepped around the clerk, who immediately began polishing the keyboard where Austin's hands had been.

On the sidewalk, Austin stuck a sourball in his cheek.

"What a big-shot scumbag," I huffed. "Why'd you let him do that?"

"Here," said Austin. He handed me a sourball. I put it in my mouth and it felt like all the spit was being vacuumed off the back of my throat.

"If you're going to be a man, little bro, you gotta turn the other cheek," said Austin.

"Why?" I chucked the sourball onto the sidewalk. "So I can get punched twice?"

Austin put a hand on my shoulder. "Little bro, you need a good dose of Jesus."

I shook him off fast. "Jesus?!" I imagined myself in shiny shoes, polishing a Bible. "Not me. No way. No how."

"Uh-huh." Austin folded his arms. "It's the ones who fight it the most who want it the worst."

"Guess again," I said.

Austin's church smelled of mildew and paint. I didn't want to be there, but Mrs. Goodwin had asked Austin to come early.

"Great echo!" I bounced my basketball. Austin gave me a look.

He sat at the piano while I doodled on visitor cards. He played quietly at first, but the music grew. It whirlpooled around me. I felt like someone had opened a door in my chest and poured the notes in. "Wow!" I said when he was done. "What was that?"

"Just something I made up."

"Beautiful!" A lady stepped in, with bracelets up and down her arms. "Austin, you make an old woman cry."

"You must be Kyle." She smiled. "Take Austin downstairs, Kyle. There's something he should see."

Downstairs was a kitchen, some scratched tables, and a couple of high chairs. Then we saw it. Against the wall was Austin's Yamaha PR-500!

"Mrs. Goodwin!" Austin let out his breath. "How did you . . . ?"

Her bracelets jingled. "You've earned it, sugar," she said. "You've washed enough windows. Now it's my turn."

"You've already—"

"Hush, boy. Let an old woman have her way."

Austin turned on the keyboard. He made it sound like a violin, he played drum rhythms, he made it sound like an angel choir.

"Hey," I asked him, "can you make it sound like it's belching?"

"Try again," said Austin.

When Austin went upstairs, I offered to baby-sit the keyboard. It was pretty cool. It could do trumpets and organ and something called "vibraphone."

Then I got an idea. If I could make a urinal play "Jingle Bells," it would be easy to move a few wires and see if I could get a cow, a sheep, and a chicken. Austin would bust a gut laughing.

I found a screwdriver and took off the back. I pulled the circuit board, messed with it, and reinstalled it. Then I pressed a key. It sounded exactly like a strangled duck. I pressed another key. Same thing. No bells, no drums . . . just a shriek ending in a puttering wheeze.

Overhead the piano stopped. There were footsteps on the stairs. I shoved wires back into the keyboard as fast as I could.

Austin burst in and stopped. He looked at my fistful of wires. Without saying a word, he jammed a sourball in his mouth and left.

I found him on his knees in the sanctuary. Mrs. Goodwin was gone.

"What are you doing?" I asked.

"I'm praying I don't kill you," he muttered through the sourball.

It was a good time to go back downstairs. I messed with more wires. Nothing worked. It wasn't my fault it had so many circuits. If Austin was going to be that way, there was no reason to stay.

There was a sour taste in my mouth as I rode the bus home.

Austin didn't show the next day. A week went by. It wasn't like I needed taking care of, but there was nothing to do. I couldn't even shoot hoops because I'd left my basketball at Austin's church.

I thought about all the basketball he'd played with me, even though he always lost. There were guys who sat with me at lunch and laughed when I made milk come out my nose, but Austin was a real friend.

And I wasn't.

I decided I really needed my basketball.

Austin was playing the church piano when I sneaked into

the sanctuary. His sad music seeped inside me. Two stupid tears dripped down my nose.

When I went to wipe them, my basketball bounced to the floor. Austin looked up. I looked down and blinked my eyes a bunch of times. He walked up the aisle and put a hand on my shoulder. This time I didn't shake him off.

"I'm sorry," I mumbled, feeling the awfulness of what I'd done. "I tried to fix it, but—" Austin nodded. "Are you . . . still mad?" How lame. He probably hated me.

"Jesus says forgive," he said. "Forgive isn't a feeling, little bro. It's something you do."

"Will you still be my buddy?" I looked up at Austin and he grinned real fast.

"Yeah," he said. "I will, little bro. There are a few things you've still gotta learn."

THE INVITATION

Mary Hollingsworth

*S*he was no ordinary music teacher. Jessica Davis, or "Ms. D" as the kids called her, cared . . . really cared about her students at Central Junior High School, where she had taught for so many years. She was more than their teacher—she was a friend, a mentor, a nurse, a counselor, and, when necessary, a fill-in mother.

Still, after twenty-six years in the classroom, what do I have to show for it? she wondered. *Tired feet. A closet full of trinkets and apple mementos. A shelf full of school annuals. And a measly retirement fund that I can't possibly live on.*

The longer she thought about it, the more she was convinced that it was time to move on. She needed to do something else with the rest of her life—something more lucrative, something where she could get the recognition she deserved, something fun, something that didn't smell like chalk dust and school cafeteria food.

She glanced down at the unsigned contract on her desk. Did she really want to sign up for yet another year of junior high kids with overactive hormones, zits, and squirmy bodies? Giggling girls who couldn't match pitch and boys whose voices were squeaking and changing?

Jessica sighed as she got up from her desk and went to her small kitchen to make a cup of her favorite raspberry tea. She always thought more clearly with a cup of tea. As she waited for the kettle to begin its song, she stared out her kitchen window. In the park across the street she saw a yellow kite with a homemade tail floating on the spring breeze. Higher and higher it rose. *That's what I want to do*, thought Jessica. *I want to fly! I don't want to be tied down anymore. I want to do what I want, when I want, where I want.*

That's what I want to do, thought Jessica. I want to fly!

Dropping the wet teabag into the trash, she took her cup of tea and walked resolutely back to her desk. She opened her desk drawer and took out a sheet of classic beige stationery, then picked up her favorite old Sheaffer fountain pen and began to write her letter of resignation to the school board.

Half an hour later, after carefully wording the letter, she folded it inside the unsigned contract and put it in the business-sized envelope she had addressed in her best penmanship.

Am I doing the right thing, Lord? she wondered. She sat for several minutes holding the envelope in her hand, staring at the washable blue ink, pondering the impact her letter would have on her life and others'. At last she rose and went to the front door. As she opened the door, she saw the postman leaving her mailbox in his white-red-and-blue truck. She had just missed him. *Oh well, tomorrow will be soon enough*, she thought.

Opening the mailbox to put her letter inside, she found a classy-looking, embossed envelope addressed to "Ms. D." She took it out and put her resignation letter in its place, raising the little red flag on the side of the mailbox. As she turned the expensive envelope over to examine it, she strolled back toward the house. The spring air was warm and wonderful, and the gentle breeze kissed her cheeks and made her smile. So she sat down in her old oak porch swing and carefully opened the letter. Pushing the swing back and forth, back and forth with one toe, she began to read:

Dear Ms. D,

You may not remember me, but I was one of your students at Central Junior High School about ten years ago. You might remember me by the nickname the other kids called me: Frumpy.

THE INVITATION

Frumpy! Sure, she remembered—an overweight girl with stringy hair and terrible skin, from a poor family, homemade clothes . . . But, oh yes, an unusual musical gift. A big, rich voice and the talent to sing with feeling and interpretation. She returned to the letter with more interest.

> I'm writing to say thank you . . . for so many things. Thank you for believing in me when no one else did. Thank you for helping me see past my acne-covered face to my real potential. Thank you for caring enough to spend extra time with me after school giving me private voice lessons . . . for free. Thank you for seeing beyond Frumpy to fine.
>
> The enclosed documents are my small way of showing my appreciation for all you did for me, whether you knew it or not. It would mean so much to me if you accept.
>
> > Blessings and thanks,
> > Jerilyn Russeau

Setting the letter aside, Jessica picked up the envelope again with curiosity. Inside she found a round-trip airline ticket to New York City and an engraved invitation on cream-colored parchment paper. The raised, gold lettering bespoke its expense and importance.

CHAPTER SIX: *Hugs Make Music* . . .

Carnegie Hall cordially invites you
to attend the debut performance of
Miss Jerilyn Russeau,
soprano, with the
New York Philharmonic Orchestra
on Saturday evening,
the twelfth of June
at eight o'clock in the evening.

Smiling with heart-bursting pride, she read the invitation again. *Frumpy at Carnegie Hall. Wow! And she thinks I helped her get there in some small way.*

As warm tears spilled out of her eyes and down her cheeks, Jessica pushed her toe down to stop the squeaking swing. She paused for several seconds, thinking. Then, getting up, she walked slowly off the porch and out to the mailbox, put the red flag down, and removed the beige letter. Turning back to the house, she glanced up and smiled at the cloudless sky.

Thank you, Lord. I got your letter.

BEAUTIFUL DREAMER

Arthur Gordon

We were broke that summer, good and broke. I had worked up enough courage to quit the magazine and try free-lancing, but I underestimated the length of time it takes to get started. Also, when you're scared you tighten up and write badly. We kept the show on the road by selling a few things—household things—at the outdoor auction on the edge of town. But that was all we did sell, and finally it got to the point where Pam decided to take the children to visit their grandmother for a while. We hadn't quarreled, or anything. It was just a question of debts, and of paying for the groceries.

She left early one morning, and I think that was the longest day of my life. I tried to work, but it was no good; the house was too quiet and empty. I kept telling myself I didn't have to endure all this, that all I had to do was call the magazine and ask for my old job back. I was pretty sure I'd get it. In the end, it wasn't courage that kept me from making that call. It was lack of it. I didn't have the nerve to admit that I had failed.

The sun went down and the twilight was gray with loneliness. When it was fully dark, I decided to walk down to the auction and sell a suitcase I had. Pam had a birthday coming up and I wanted to buy her a present.

It wasn't much of a place, really, just a big shed full of junk, and a tent with folding chairs where people came to bid for things you'd have thought nobody could possibly want. Secondhand things, castoffs—even broken things.

The owner was a hard-bitten little gnome named Willie Madden who looked at the world suspiciously from under a green eyeshade and from behind a dead cigar. He and Pam had gotten pretty chummy over our previous transactions, but I didn't like him much.

I arranged to have the suitcase auctioned. Then, since there was an hour to kill, I prowled around looking at the old furniture and chipped china and musty books. And finally, near the back of the shed, I noticed a young couple standing close together and whispering about something.

They were not a very striking pair; neither of them was tall and the girl wasn't particularly pretty. But there was something nice and close about them. They were inspecting a secondhand baby carriage, and it was obvious that before long they were going to need one.

"Well, go and ask him," the girl said, loud enough for me to hear. "You can ask, can't you?"

The boy nodded and went away. While he was gone, the girl stood looking down at the carriage. In its prime it had been quite a fancy affair, and it was still in good condition. I saw her stroke the ivory handle gently, and once she bent and reexamined the price tag, as if she hoped somehow her first impression of what it read had been wrong.

Her husband came back presently with Willie Madden. Willie grunted at me from under his eyeshade, then went over and looked at the tag himself. "That's right," he said. "Twenty-five bucks. An absolute steal at that price, too. It's worth fifty."

The girl asked a question, her face wistful as she looked at the carriage.

"Well, bring it in, bring it in," Willie said impatiently. "Bring in anything you want to get rid of. But you better hurry. I got to be up on that platform in just forty-five minutes."

The youngsters hurried away, but in twenty minutes they were back. I watched them go up to Willie's cluttered desk and put down the things they were carrying: a fishing rod, a couple of dresses, an alarm clock, and a few other odds and ends including something that looked like a music box. It didn't look like twenty-five dollars' worth of auctionable stuff to me, and I knew it didn't to Willie. He poked at the music box with one skeptical finger. "This thing work?"

"It plays one tune," the girl said. "It's supposed to play three but it plays one."

Willie's cigar revolved slowly. "I paid twenty-two bucks for that carriage. Here it is, right in the book. If we can get that much for this stuff of yours, you can have it. But I tell you right now, I don't think you'll get that much. So don't say I didn't warn you. Go on, now; wait in the tent. I got things to do."

I sat where I could watch their faces. They held hands and waited.

They went, and I followed them. I sat where I could watch their faces. They held hands and waited. Somebody got a good buy on my suitcase; it went for fourteen dollars, and was worth forty. The youngsters' things were at the end of the list; it was late when Willie got around to them. The fishing rod brought three dollars, the dresses two each, the alarm clock, fifty cents. It was hopeless, absolutely hopeless. I tried not to look at them.

Willie picked up the music box. "Now this here," he said, "is a genuine antique. What's more, it really plays. Listen."

He pressed the lever. The box gave a faint purring sound; then it played. The song was Stephen Foster's "Beautiful Dreamer." It came tinkling out, slow and sad, the most haunting of all American folk songs, maybe of folk songs anywhere:

170

BEAUTIFUL DREAMER

Beautiful dreamer, wake unto me,
Starlight and dewdrop are waiting for thee.

The tent was very still. The music went on, thin and clear and sweet, and somehow everything was in it—all the loneliness and the heartache and the things all of us want to say and never find the words. I looked at the young couple, and something in their faces made my throat feel tight.

The music stopped. "Well," said Willie, "what am I bid? Ten dollars? Anyone bid ten dollars?"

Silence again. I thought of the fourteen dollars I would be getting for my suitcase. Less commission. I thought about Pam and her birthday, too.

"Anybody bid five?" Willie sounded impatient. "Anybody bid five dollars for this genuine antique?"

I took a deep breath, opened my mouth and then miserably closed it again.

"Five dollars!" said a voice behind me. I looked around. It was a thin, shabby man with a carefully waxed mustache. I had seen him at auctions before, but I had never heard him bid on anything.

Even Willie seemed rather surprised. "Fi-dollazime bid . . . who'll make it ten? Ten dollars? Who'll make it eight?"

"Eight!" It was a little birdlike woman on the far side of the tent.

Every eye in the place swung back to the shabby man. He did not even hesitate. "Ten dollars!"

"Twelve!" cried his rival. She looked as if she didn't have twelve cents.

"Twelve I'm bid," yelled Willie. "Do I hear fifteen?"

There was a hush that seemed to go on forever. Fifteen dollars would do it for them, plus the money from their other things. The girl was very pale; she was holding her husband's hand so tightly that I saw him wince.

The shabby man stood up slowly. "Fifteen dollars!" he said with grand finality.

That did it. The music box was going—it was gone—sold to the gentleman with the mustache. For a moment the grim thought occurred to me that the gentleman might not have fifteen dollars. But no, he produced the money, gave it to Willie's assistant, took the box.

When the tent was empty, I went back into the shed. The baby carriage, I was glad to note, was gone. I collected my suitcase money and decided to treat myself to a cup of coffee. The truth was I didn't want to go back to my empty house. I went into the diner across the street and stopped just inside the door. The little birdlike lady and her rival with the mustache were sitting there, side by side, on a couple of stools.

I understood the whole thing, then. I went up to them and said sharply, as if I had a right to know, "Where's the music box?"

The owner of the mustache looked faintly startled. "The box?" he said. "Why, Willie's got it."

I turned to his companion. "How much did Willie pay you to bid against each other?"

She dunked a doughnut daintily. "Why, nothing," she said. "We were glad to do it, weren't we, Henry?"

"I suppose," I said, "that it was Willie's money you used to pay for it too."

"Sure," said Henry. "Where would I get fifteen bucks for a music box? Willie just hates for people to know what a softie he is, that's all."

I left them there and went back to the shed where Willie sat at his desk. I guess he wore that eyeshade to make himself look tough. "Where's the box?" I asked.

He stared me right in the eye. "What box?"

"Come on, Willie," I said. "I know what you did. Where is it?"

The eyeshade moved an inch to the left. "In the cupboard there. Why?"

"I want you to hold it for me. I'll give you twenty bucks for it when I have the money."

Willie leaned back in his chair. "Now just what," he said, "would you do with that box?"

"I'd give it to Pam for her birthday."

Willie shook his head. "Are you crazy? It's not worth five bucks, let alone twenty. It only plays one tune. It's supposed to play three."

"I like the tune it does play," I told him. "There's a lot of love in it."

"Love?" said Willie. He got up slowly and came around the desk. He looked at me balefully. "Why don't you get a job and do some work for a change? Why don't you quit this fool way of living?"

I just laughed out loud. I felt happy and warm and good inside. I knew that sooner or later everything would be all right.

Willie opened the cupboard. "Here." He held out the box. "Give it to Pam. On her birthday. From me."

I hesitated for a second; then I took it. There are times when it is selfish to refuse a gift. "Thanks."

"Well, go on home," said Willie. "I can't stand around here all night talking."

So I went home. The house was still dark and empty, but I put the box on the table by our bed. I put it there, and I let it play, and I wasn't lonely anymore.

RECAPTURE THE WONDER

Ravi Zacharias

*T*here is a story I have told before that I would like to tell again, because there is a marvelous sequel to it. The people I mention are true heroes. They make our world a better place and show the world what wonder is all about, blending reality with a sacred imagination. They live in Connecticut, and several years ago they read of a little boy in Romania who was born without arms, not even an appendage on either shoulder. When he was about one year old they visited the orphanage where he was being cared for because his parents were unable to, and their hearts went out to him. Most of the caregivers in that orphanage would have no more than minimal contact with him because they feared the "evil eye" represented by his deformity and the bad luck they believed he would bring them.

Through discussion and contacts, this couple asked if they could adopt this little one. The boy's mother, as well as many

175

others, questioned the motives of anyone who would take him into their lives and spend themselves in this way, caring for one in such need of nurture and assistance. She asked, "Are you taking him to America so you can use him for experiments? I have heard that they do that in America." Mike and Sharon assured her that this was not their intent at all. They just wanted to give him a home and a chance at life.

"But why would you want a baby like mine?" the mother asked. Sharon had had the foresight to bring a Romanian Bible with her, and opening it to Psalm 139, she gave it to the Romanian mother to read for herself:

> For you created my inmost being;
>> you knit me together in my mother's womb.
> I praise you because I am fearfully and wonderfully made;
>> your works are wonderful,
>> I know that full well.
> My frame was not hidden from you
>> When I was made in the secret place.
>> —Psalm 139:13–15

As the mother read from God's Word, tears started to stream down her face. Finally she looked at Sharon and said, "If this is what you believe about my son, you can have him as yours."

RECAPTURE THE WONDER

Sharon and Mike brought him back home, where they have loved him and raised him. He learned to use his feet to hold his spoon and feed himself. In every restaurant he and they became the topic of conversation as people marveled at the gift given to him in these parents, the fascinating skill in his feet, but most of all, at his lovable face and sweet personality.

Here is the sequel. Young George is now eight years old. Sharon decided to have a caring

If this is what you believe about my son, you can have him as yours.

Christian teacher train him in playing a classical instrument. You can imagine the hard work and the patience demanded by parents and teacher in such a venture. Naturally, he had to learn to play it with his feet. Some time ago came the first recital and they wondered whether to put him on the program with all the other students. The teacher said she would want him in the program and she would sit next to him as he played. May I just quote the words the father sent to me in a letter? I wept when I read it, and I suspect you will too.

The big night came, and George was nervous and telling us he wasn't so sure if he wanted to do this . . . to make matters worse, there was a much bigger crowd of people than normal for one of these events . . . many of whom had never seen

George or met George before. Several students went up to the front and played their various pieces, and very soon it was time. . . . George's name was called. You could have heard a pin drop as the teacher walked up with him, carrying his instrument, a chair and a large pillow that she placed on the floor to lift up the neck of the cello. She arranged everything as he needed and nodded for him to go ahead.

There was a feeling of wonder and tension in the room, and at this point my only thought was, "Please, Lord, let him just get through this . . . ," George began, and the very first note he struck was as sour as could be! He stopped playing, got red in the face, shrugged his shoulders, broke into a huge grin and looked up at the teacher. She warmly smiled back and nodded to him that he should try again.

Well, George then proceeded to play the entire song without a flaw, and it sounded marvelous. When he finished, there was a moment of quiet, and then one of the older students (who is the most advanced student in the group) simply stood in his place and began to clap. Many others in the audience stood to their feet and the applause went on for a very long time. . . . My wife turned to me and said, "George has never once, before tonight, made it through that song without many mistakes!"

Then Mike added these words: "What a great picture of our relationship with our heavenly Father! We are weak, nervous, afraid and flawed and yet Christ stands beside us and warmly says, 'And surely I am with you always to the very end of the age.' God does not hear our sour notes but only the unflawed music and perfection of His perfect Son."

This, may I suggest, is the picture of wonder from every side. The sacred imagination of a young couple, which is greater than the glory of the stars, I might add; the power to inspire a weak young life, not merely to fly on a wing but to play music without any arms; the heartfelt commitment of a teacher who brought music into his heart not merely as a means to cope with life but to celebrate life; the applause of those who recognized what had been accomplished, not merely to be happy for him but to be awe-stricken; the tears of gratitude at the smile of a little life that gloried in the affirmation of those who loved him and gave him this gift. I have to wonder what his biological mother would have said had she been there. Psalm 139 would have now not just been read but heard and seen as well.

There is a postscript. This young family has now adopted a young lad from India with the same handicap. George now has a brother, just as unique as he is but from a different part of the world. The wonder expands.

CHAPTER SIX: *Hugs Make Music* . . .

There is wonder all around us, and it is God's will to fill us with that wonder that makes life enchanting and sacred. We cannot help but sing when that happens. Maybe that is why, of all the religions in the world, there is none with the wealth of music that the Christian faith offers. We sing because His name is "Wonderful." But how do we find this wonder, not merely in His name but in such as way that our heart rests in that delight? We hope the answer is not as elusive as the world has made it to be.

THE DUET

Charlotte Greeson

Vicki Graham and I have been best friends since we were two years old—more than sixty years now (which neither of us can imagine!). We grew up together in Sulphur, Oklahoma, on the edge of Platt National Park. Our parents were best friends at church, and we lived across the street from each other.

Vicki and I were as different as night and day. I was a princess; she was a cowgirl. I loved to stay inside and read; she wanted to go outside and play. I liked to wear dresses; she wore boots and jeans. But there were three things we both liked: playing the piano, riding horses, and each other. We took piano lessons from the same teacher for several years when we were in grade school, and the teacher often had us play duets for recitals and programs. We loved playing together, and it was something we continued to do for fun for many years.

181

CHAPTER SIX: *Hugs Make Music . . .*

Vicki stopped taking piano when she got out of grade school, but I continued taking all through high school and college. Eventually I became a music teacher, which I've now done for about forty years. Vicki went on to become editor of the local newspaper, mayor of Sulphur, a published author, and a licensed counselor. But back to my story.

We also both had our own horses when we were young, and we loved to ride. We rode in parades around the area and for local events. And we spent hours and hours out exploring the creeks and forests together on our four-legged friends. Sometimes we took a picnic and stayed out the entire day together (you could do that safely in those "good old days"). This, too, was a habit we continued for several years.

About 1958, when we were in high school, Vicki accidentally got her hand caught in her horse's bridle, and when the horse yanked hard on the bridle, it pulled off half of Vicki's index finger on her left hand, leaving her with one finger that was only half as long as the others. Fortunately, she recovered well from the accident—so well, in fact, that she often forgot about having a short finger at all.

One day in 1959 we were at Vicki's house just hanging out together, as high school girls do. And we decided to see if we could still play some of the old duets we had learned in grade school. We

THE DUET

hadn't played any duets in several years, and we thought it would be fun to try. So we sat down side by side on the piano bench as we had done so many times before. I sat on the left, because I played the two-handed bass part of the duet. Vicki sat on the right, because she played

> *We hadn't played any duets in several years, and we thought it would be fun to try.*

the top two hands on this particular song. It was a fairly upbeat piece of music. Vicki's part had a dominant two-handed run of the scales in the middle of the song, while my part was the quieter rhythmic bottom notes.

When we came to Vicki's run, I was concentrating hard on my bass part when suddenly Vicki's part stopped, and I glanced over to see what was wrong. Then I stopped short. No Vicki! She had fallen off the piano bench and was lying on her back on the floor with a stunned look on her face.

"What happened?" I gasped.

Then she started laughing. She laughed so hard she couldn't talk, so she simply held up her left hand to show me her half finger. She had been so engrossed in playing the duet that she had forgotten about her short finger. About halfway through the run of her scales, her short, left index finger missed the piano key, throwing her completely off balance and onto the floor.

CHAPTER SIX: *Hugs Make Music* . . .

We laughed so hard that we never did finish the song, and we still get a kick out of remembering our notorious nineteen-and-a-half-finger duet to this day.

We're best friends for life . . . and that's the long and the short of it!

CHAPTER SEVEN

——⟨⟩——

Hugs Create Joy in the Heart

*The people who influenced
us are those who have stood
unconsciously for the right thing;
they are like the stars and the lilies,
and the joy of God flows through
them all the time.*

OSWALD CHAMBERS

ONE PERSON

Compiled from Public Facts

r. Frank Mayfield was touring Tewksbury Institute when, on his way out, he accidentally collided with an elderly floor maid. To cover the awkward moment, Dr. Mayfield started asking questions. "How long have you worked here?"

"I've worked here almost since the place opened," the maid replied.

"What can you tell me about the history of the place?" he asked.

"I don't think I can tell you anything, but I could show you something."

With that, she took his hand and led him down to the basement under the oldest section of the building. She pointed to one of what looked like small prison cells, their iron bars rusted with age, and said, "That's the cage where they used to keep Annie."

"Who's Annie?" the doctor asked.

"Annie was a young girl who was brought in here because she was wild. Nobody could do anything with her. She'd bite and scream and throw her food at people. I used to see her and think, 'I sure would hate to be locked up in a cage like that.' I wanted to help her, but I didn't have any idea what I could do.

I used to see her and think, "I sure would hate to be locked up in a cage like that." I wanted to help her.

"So one day I baked her some brownies and brought them in. I walked carefully to her cage and said, 'Annie, I baked these brownies just for you. I'll put them right here on the floor and you can come and get them if you want.' Then I got out of there as fast as I could because I was afraid she might throw them at me.

"After that, she was just a little bit nicer to me. And sometimes I would talk to her. Once, I even got her laughing. The doctors asked me if I'd help with Annie when they examined her. That is how they discovered that Annie was almost blind.

"After about a year, Annie went to the Perkins Institute for the Blind and later became a teacher. When she asked the director at Tewksbury if she could help in any way, he remembered a letter he had received. The writer was a man whose daughter was blind and very uncontrollable. He had written to ask if there was anyone who could help teach his daughter. And that is how Annie Sullivan became the lifelong companion of Helen Keller."

The doctor then remembered a statement Helen Keller made when she received the Nobel Prize. She had been asked who had the greatest impact on her life. She said Annie Sullivan. But Annie said, "No, Helen. The woman who had the greatest influence on both our lives was a floor maid at the Tewksbury Institute."

A BOX OF BROKEN DREAMS

Florence Littauer

During Christmas vacation of my senior year in college, my father took me into the den one afternoon and told me how proud he was of my achievements in speech and English. He reached in behind the piano and brought out a box of clippings he had kept hidden from the family. They were articles and letters he had written and sent to newspapers. There was even a response from Senator Henry Cabot Lodge to some advice Father had sent him. I asked him why he hadn't shown me these before. He responded that Mother had told him since he didn't have any education he shouldn't try to write. If he tried and failed, we'd all be humiliated.

At that moment I realized, in spite of all my father had taught me, I had never given him much credit for knowing anything. Like my mother, I had always felt that he didn't have the education necessary to be a success. In the past I had downgraded his ability and he had wisely waited until I was mature enough to share his hidden hobby.

Warmly, we discussed our mutual love of English and for the first time he shared that he had always wanted to be a politician. We laughed over how, when I was a child, he had made me sit and listen to political speeches on the radio.

As we discussed these and other subjects, Father brought the conversation back to his secret writing and he told me in confidence that he had sent an article to the editor of *Advance* magazine a few months before concerning the methods used in selecting delegates to our denominational

> *He had wisely waited until I was mature enough to share his hidden hobby.*

conventions. He had looked each time the issue had come to see if his article had been published.

So far it had not been included and he said, "I guess I tried for something too big this time. Your mother is right. I don't have any talent."

About suppertime we looked out the window and saw Mother get off the bus alone. When she came in we asked where Father was. "Your father is dead," she said simply. She didn't cry. She just told us the story as we stood by in shock.

They had spent a beautiful day together, and as they were walking through Park Street subway station, Father suddenly grabbed his heart and dropped to the cement. She said a nurse had been in the crowd of pushing people and knelt down to check him. She looked up at Mother and said, "He's dead," then slipped into a subway car and was gone. Mother told us how she just stood there in disbelief as busy commuters stepped over Father's form and went their way. A priest came by as a lone Good Samaritan and said, "I'll call the police," and disappeared. For over an hour Mother kept watch over the body of her husband as indifferent people pushed and tripped around him.

She then told us how she had sat beside him in the ambulance, stayed with him in the emergency room where he was officially pronounced dead, and then had to take another lonesome ride to the city morgue where the man on duty had her go through Father's pockets and remove his belongings. After all this trauma, Mother took a bus from the morgue to North Station, the train to Haverhill, and then another bus home. She had faced the tragedy bravely and alone. As Mother told the tale, customers came in and listened, and soon we were all crying together.

The morning of the funeral, as I was going through the mail and reading the day's sympathy cards, I noticed the new issue of *Advance*, January 1949. As I glanced over it I discovered to my surprise that my father's article entitled "For More Democracy" was in print. It had come too late for him to see, and had he not chosen to share his secret ambition a few days before, I would never have looked in that issue of *Advance*.

We would have missed this fulfillment of Father's humble dream.

LET'S GO BUG HUNTING

Barbara Chesser

*O*ne fall afternoon I rushed home from the university where
I taught. I prepared a hasty dinner, threatened my nine-
year-old daughter, Christi, to hurry and finish her homework "or
else," and properly reprimanded Del, my husband, for leaving his
dusty shoes on the good carpet. I then frantically vacuumed the
entryway because a group of prestigious ladies were coming by to
pick up some good used clothing for a worthwhile cause; and then
later a graduate student would be at our house to work on a very
important thesis—one that I was certain would make a sound
contribution to research.

As I paused to catch my breath, I heard Christi talking with
a friend on the telephone. Her comments went something like
this: "Mom is cleaning house—some ladies we don't even know
are coming by to pick up some old worn-out clothes . . . and a
college student is coming out to work on a thesis . . . No, I don't

LET'S GO BUG HUNTING

know what a thesis is . . . I just know Mom isn't doing anything important, and she won't go bug hunting with me."

> *Mom isn't doing anything important, and she won't go bug hunting with me.*

Before Christi had hung up the phone, I had put on my jeans and old tennis shoes, persuaded Del to do likewise, pinned a note to the door telling the graduate student I'd be back soon, and set the box of used clothing on the front porch with a note on it that Del, Christi, and I had gone bug hunting.

A STORY FOR VALENTINE'S DAY

Jo Ann Larsen

Larry and Jo Ann were an ordinary couple. They lived in an ordinary house on an ordinary street. Like any other ordinary couple, they struggled to make ends meet and to do the right things for their children.

They were ordinary in yet another way—they had their squabbles. Much of their conversation concerned what was wrong in their marriage and who was to blame.

Until one day when a most extraordinary event took place.

"You know, Jo Ann, I've got a magic chest of drawers. Every time I open them, they're full of socks and underwear," Larry said. "I want to thank you for filling them all these years."

Jo Ann stared at her husband over the top of her glasses. "What do you want, Larry?"

"Nothing. I just want you to know I appreciate those magic drawers."

A Story for Valentine's Day

This wasn't the first time Larry had done something odd, so Jo Ann pushed the incident out of her mind until a few days later.

"Jo Ann, thank you for recording so many correct check numbers in the ledger this month. You put down the right numbers 15 out of 16 times. That's a record."

Disbelieving what she had heard, Jo Ann looked up from her mending. "Larry, you're always complaining about my recording the wrong check numbers. Why stop now?"

"No reason. I just wanted you to know I appreciate the effort you're making."

Jo Ann shook her head and went back to her mending. "What's got into him?" she mumbled to herself.

Nevertheless, the next day when Jo Ann wrote a check at the grocery store, she glanced at her checkbook to confirm that she had put down the right check number. "Why do I suddenly care about those dumb check numbers?" she asked herself.

She tried to disregard the incident, but Larry's strange behavior intensified.

"Jo Ann, that was a great dinner," he said one evening. "I appreciate all your effort. Why, in the past fifteen years I'll bet you've fixed over 14,000 meals for me and the kids."

Then "Gee, Jo Ann, the house looks spiffy. You've really worked hard to get it looking so good." And even, "Thanks, Jo Ann, for just being you. I really enjoy your company."

Jo Ann was growing worried. "Where's the sarcasm, the criticism?" she wondered.

Her fears that something peculiar was happening to her husband were confirmed by sixteen-year-old Shelly, who complained, "Dad's gone bonkers, Mom. He just told me I looked nice. With all this makeup and these sloppy clothes, he still said it. That's not Dad, Mom. What's wrong with him?"

Whatever was wrong, Larry didn't get over it. Day in and day out he continued focusing on the positive.

Larry didn't get over it. Day in and day out he continued focusing on the positive.

Over the weeks, Jo Ann grew more accustomed to her mate's unusual behavior and occasionally even gave him a grudging "Thank you." She prided herself on taking it all in stride, until one day something so peculiar happened, she became completely discombobulated:

"I want you to take a break," Larry said. "I am going to do the dishes. So please take your hands off that frying pan and leave the kitchen."

(Long, long pause.) "Thank you, Larry. Thank you very much!"

Jo Ann's step was now a little lighter, her self-confidence higher and once in a while she hummed. She didn't seem to have as many blue moods anymore. "I rather like Larry's new behavior," she thought.

That would be the end of the story except one day another most extraordinary event took place. This time it was Jo Ann who spoke.

"Larry," she said, "I want to thank you for going to work and providing for us all these years. I don't think I've ever told you how much I appreciate it."

Larry has never revealed the reason for his dramatic change of behavior no matter how hard Jo Ann has pushed for an answer, and so it will likely remain one of life's mysteries. But it's one I'm thankful to live with.

You see, I am Jo Ann.

Dinner-Plate Dahlias

Melodie M. Davis

Aunt Mae's home was tucked at the very end of a mountain hollow, the term folks use to describe the V-shaped winding pass in and through low-lying Appalachian mountains. Flowers—annuals and perennials alike—grew in every smidgen of spare dirt at Aunt Mae's place, and in every old pot or pan she could put to that use.

A long-stemmed gourd hung on the wall of a shed, a woodbox on the porch held fuel for the kitchen cook stove; a well-kept outhouse sat a discreet distance from the house. There was even an old, natural spring with a cupboard built over the top. Wild ferns and potted wandering Jews placed artfully around the spring made it more than just a place to draw drinking water; it looked like a place to find the kind of "living water" Jesus offered to the woman at the well.

In late summer, the impatiens spread out like small bushes,

coleus flourished in dark greens and rich reds, and dinner-plate dahlias grew as big as their name predicts.

Aunt Mae and Uncle George raised chickens for a living until technology shut them out of the increasingly competitive poultry world. They could not afford to make the improvements on their poultry house required by the producer with whom they contracted. Taking care of chickens keeps you close to home— family reunions used to be planned around "when George's chickens are sold." That way Mae and George wouldn't have to worry about electrical storms turning off the fans in the chicken house on a sweltering August Sunday.

How could anyone living in our time be happy with as little as Aunt Mae had?

Of course, there was much about my husband's aunt I really didn't know. When she succumbed to cancer at the not-so-old age of sixty-eight, I wondered if Aunt Mae was happy back that long lane, a mile from the nearest road, eighteen miles from the nearest town. How could anyone living in our time be happy with as little as Aunt Mae had?

At her funeral in a little knotty-pine church, the sanctuary was full; I didn't know she even knew so many people. But that was my ignorance. At the dinner held after her funeral, I puttered around her yard, breathing in the beauty and tranquillity of what a real estate ad might call "a mountain Eden." I decided Aunt Mae must have been happy, if flowers and friends and family and faith in God can fill one with joy.

I'm sure she had her disappointments like all of us, and great frustration in battling cancer over several years and numerous operations. But one lesson I'm trying to absorb from Aunt Mae is her apparent joy in the simple things of life.

It's not wrong to have big visions, to have great ideas about what you want to accomplish and dreams for your children. But so often goals and aspirations—our dreams of "making it big"—block out real appreciation for all that we already enjoy.

There was a nice but not extravagant number of flower arrangements lining the entrance to the church at her funeral. There were probably more store-bought flowers than Aunt Mae had ever received in her life, but somehow the luxury seemed appropriate. How else would you celebrate the life of this green thumb than by offering up lots of beautiful bouquets? Flowers ask so little of life; they just make the world a prettier place during their short existence.

Do you know any "Aunt Maes"? You know, those saints whose main gift to the world was that they taught others how to appreciate life, and maybe know a little more of God?

A LITTLE GOOD NEWS

M. Norvel Young

One cold evening I came in off our balcony that overlooks the Pacific Ocean. I clicked on the television for the evening news. To my delight, the news commentator was telling a heartwarming story—some *good* news for a change.

Tom Nichter had seventy-five cents in his pocket that Thursday evening in February—all that stood between his family and hunger. They were homeless, living in their old car. He and his wife, Pauline, had been jobless for months because of cutbacks at their work. Bills were mounting mercilessly.

Pauline remembered, "We were at the lowest point in our lives that evening. We were out of work, out of money, and had no place to live. We were pretty much out of hope too."

Tom and Pauline's eleven-year-old son, Jason, wanted to go to the mall just to look around. So they went. Pauline waited while Jason ran up and down the aisles of the toy store pointing out games to his dad. She was looking around idly when she saw a gray leather folder, like a big wallet, on top of a stack of games. She took another look and noticed there seemed to be money inside. She remembered thinking, *It must be play money*, as she picked up the wallet. She was shocked to see that the money was *real* . . . and there was a lot of it.

Pauline showed Tom and Jason the wallet. "Could this be meant for us?" She and Tom thought briefly of all the ways they could put that money to use. It appeared to be two or three thousand dollars—a small fortune to them. They quickly decided, though, that the money was not theirs, and they didn't want to set a bad example for Jason. So, they closed the wallet and looked for a security guard.

When they couldn't find a guard, they drove several miles, using up their precious gasoline, to take the wallet to the Buena Park police station. When they entered, Sergeant Terry Branum was talking to Jay Schermerhorn, a KNBC-TV cameraman who was at the station. Pauline placed the wallet on the counter in front of Sergeant Branum and said, "We found this at the mall. We don't even really know what's in it."

Sergeant Branum was surprised to find credit cards, a passport, a fifteen-hundred-dollar plane ticket, and $2,394 in cash. Tom was amazed that it was so much money. The sergeant asked Tom to tell him the story. Slowly, Tom described their situation and how they had come to find the wallet. He related how he had been looking for a steady job for over two years. Then, a year ago, Pauline's division of her company was closed too. Despite an excellent work record, she had been unable to find employment since.

Schermerhorn stood by, taking in the station drama. He suggested to Sergeant Branum that they do an interview when the wallet owner was found. The officer called the mall and was told that the owner had just come in to report the lost wallet.

In twenty minutes, a relieved tourist reclaimed his wallet and its contents as the

The Nichters' story of honesty and goodness made page one.

TV camera recorded the scene. The man thanked the Nichters profusely, but he offered no reward. Later that night the Nichters were out eating hamburgers (on three dollars given to them by Sergeant Branum) while we watched their story on the evening news.

The next morning reporter Erin Kelly of the *Orange County Register* called the police station to find out if anything newsworthy had happened. Sergeant Branum told her about the Nichters.

"That's a *great* story!" said Kelly excitedly. "The whole paper is just dead bodies today, and I'd love to print some good news."

The Nichters' story of honesty and goodness made page one. It was also picked up by the wire services and spread to media all over the U.S.

and abroad. Theirs was the "good deed heard 'round the world." The police station was soon overwhelmed with people calling who wanted to help the Nichters. Calls came in from as far away as Toronto, London, and Istanbul. One person walked into the police station and asked how much money had been in the wallet. When Sergeant Branum told him, he wrote a check for $2,400, handed it to the officer and said, "They deserve at least that."

By the next Monday, mail was pouring into the police station from everywhere. Some days it took six people eight full hours just to open the envelopes. Inside were good wishes, prayers, and donations from fifty cents to hundreds of dollars. Everyone wanted to help the Nichters get back on their feet and reward their good deed.

Our local businesses took up collections and dropped off boxes filled with canned goods, paper products, and toiletries. The family received a bed for Jason, airline tickets to anywhere they wanted to go in the U.S., and many other things they needed so badly. A realtor even offered them six months' free rent in an apartment she owned in Garden Grove. And job offers came for both Tom and Pauline from all over.

The Nichters were amazed at the response to their act and absolutely overwhelmed by the goodness of people. "After all," said Tom, "we didn't do anything special. We only did the *right* thing."

THE WRONG ONE

Tony Campolo

One afternoon, as I sat in my office, the telephone rang. It was my mother. She told me that Mrs. Kirkpatrick had died and that the least I could do was to go to the funeral. My mother, like all Italians, was big on funerals. She felt that it was of enormous importance to show "respect" and honor the deceased with our presence. So, while I was growing up I attended more funerals than I can remember out of "respect." However, in Mrs. Kirkpatrick's case, it was more than respect that made me say yes to my mother's request. Mrs. Kirkpatrick was a lovely lady, and as we were growing up she did many wonderful things for the children of our church. I could always count on her giving me candy at Christmastime. On one occasion she took me to a concert so that I could hear a symphony orchestra play. Mrs. Kirkpatrick had added much to my life, and my mother was right. Going to her funeral was the least I could do to show respect and appreciation.

CHAPTER SEVEN: *Hugs Create Joy . . .*

I arrived at the funeral home at two o'clock, just as the funeral was scheduled to begin. I rushed up the steps and hurried by the somber man at the door. There were several funerals in progress at the time. I walked into what I thought was the designated room for Mrs. Kirkpatrick's funeral and quickly took a seat. I had done it so hurriedly, I failed to notice that, other than an elderly woman sitting two seats away from me, there

I looked over the edge of the casket, and he did not look like Mrs. Kirkpatrick!

was no one else in the entire room. I looked over the edge of the casket, and *he* did not look like Mrs. Kirkpatrick! I had the wrong funeral! I was just about to leave when the woman reached over and grabbed me by the arm, and with desperation in her voice said, "You *were* his friend—weren't you?"

I didn't know what to say. Dietrich Bonhoeffer, the famous German martyr, once said, "There comes a time in every man's life when he must lie with imagination, with vigor and with enthusiasm!" I don't know whether you concur with Bonhoeffer, but just for the record, you should know that I lied. What else could I do? The woman was reaching out for assurance that somebody had some connection with her husband and some concern for her. What was I to say? "I'm sorry, I'm at the wrong funeral. Your husband didn't have any friends." She needed to know that there was somebody to whom her husband meant something. And so I lied and said I knew him, and that he was always kind to me.

I went through the funeral sitting at her side. Afterward, the two of us went out and got into the sole automobile that would follow the hearse to the cemetery. I figured that since I had gone that far, I might as well go all the way. I wasn't about to leave this poor old lady alone in her hour of deep sadness.

We stood at the edge of the grave and said some prayers. As the casket was lowered into the grave, each of us threw a flower onto it. We then got back into the car and returned to the funeral home. As we arrived there, I took this elderly woman's hand and said to her, "Mrs. King, I have to tell you something. I really did not know your husband. I want to be your friend, and I can't be your friend after today unless I tell you the truth. I did not know your husband. I came to the funeral by mistake."

I waited a long while wondering how she would respond. She held my hand for what seemed an interminable moment, then answered, "You'll never ever, ever know how much your being with me meant to me today."

I know there will be those who will say I should never have lied to this woman in the first place. But then, they weren't there. I had a feeling at the end of that day that there was a voice within me, speaking to me and saying, "Well done, thou good and faithful servant!"

CHAPTER EIGHT

***

Hugs Are Touches of the Heart

If I can put one touch of

a rosy sunset into the life of any

man or woman, I shall feel that

I have worked with God.

G. K. CHESTERTON

MY FIRST CHRISTMAS TREE

Hamlin Garland

J will begin by saying that we never had a Christmas tree in our house in the Wisconsin coulee; indeed, my father never saw one in a family circle till he saw that which I set up for my own children last year. But we celebrated Christmas in those days, always, and I cannot remember a time when we did not all hang up our stockings for "Sandy Claws" to fill. As I look back upon those days it seems as if the snows were always deep, the night skies crystal clear, and the stars especially lustrous with frosty sparkles of blue and yellow fire—and probably this was so, for we lived in a Northern land where winter was usually stern and always long.

I recall one Christmas when "Sandy" brought me a sled, and a horse that stood on rollers—a wonderful tin horse which I very shortly split in two in order to see what his insides were. Father traded a cord of wood for the sled, and the horse cost twenty cents—but they made the day wonderful.

Another notable Christmas Day, as I stood in our front yard, mid-leg deep in snow, a neighbor drove by closely muffled in furs, while behind his seat his son, a lad of twelve or fifteen, stood beside a barrel of apples, and as he passed he hurled a glorious big red one at me. It missed me, but bored a deep, round hole in the soft snow. I thrill yet with the remembered joy of burrowing for that delicious bomb. Nothing will ever smell quite as good as that Wine Sap or Northern Spy or whatever it was. It was a wayward impulse on the part of the boy on the sleigh, but it warms my heart after more than forty years.

We had no chimney in our home, but the stocking-hanging was a ceremony nevertheless. My parents, and especially my mother, entered into it with the best of humor. They always put up their own stockings or permitted us to do it for them—and they always laughed next morning when they found potatoes or ears of corn in them. I can see now that my mother's laugh had a tear in it, for she loved pretty things and seldom got any during the years that we lived in the coulée.

When I was ten years old we moved to Mitchell Country, an Iowa prairie land, and there we prospered in such wise that our stockings always held toys of some sort, and even my mother's stocking occasionally sagged with a simple piece of jewelry or a new comb or brush. But the thought of a family tree remained the luxury of millionaire city dwellers; indeed, it was not till my fifteenth or sixteenth year that our Sunday school rose to the extravagance of a tree, and it is of this wondrous festival that I write.

The land about us was only partly cultivated at this time, and our district schoolhouse, a bare little box, was set bleakly on the prairie; but the Burr Oak schoolhouse was not only larger but it stood beneath great oaks as well and possessed the charm of a forest background through which a stream ran silently. It was our chief social center. There of a Sunday a regular preacher held "Divine service" with Sunday school as a sequence. At night—usually on Friday nights—the young people let in "ly-ceums," as we called them, to debate great questions or to "speak pieces" and read essays; and here it was that I saw my first Christmas tree.

I walked to that tree across four miles of moonlit snow. Snow? No, it was a floor of diamonds, a magical world, so beautiful that my heart still aches with the wonder of it and with the regret that it has all gone—gone with the keen eyes and the bounding pulses of the boy.

Our home at this time was a small frame house on the prairie almost directly west of the Burr Oak grove. As it was too cold to take the horses out, my brother and I, with our tall boots, our visored caps and our long woolen mufflers, started forth afoot defiant of the cold. We left the gate on the trot, bound for a sight of the glittering unknown. The snow was deep and we moved side by side in the grooves made by the hoofs of the horses, setting our feet in the shine left by the broad shoes of the wood sleighs whose going had smoothed the way for us.

Our breaths rose like smoke in the still air. It must have been ten below zero, but that did not trouble us in those days, and at last we came in sight of the lights, in sound of the singing, the laughter, the bells of the feast.

I stood against the wall and gazed with open-eyed marveling at the shining pine.

It was a poor little building without tower or bell and its low walls had but three windows on a side, and yet it seemed very imposing to me that night as I crossed the threshold and faced the strange people who packed it to the door. I say "strange people," for though I had seen most of them many times they all seemed somehow alien to me that night. I was an irregular attendant at Sunday school and did not expect a present; therefore I stood against the wall and gazed with open-eyed marveling at the shining pine which stood where the pulpit was wont to be. I was made to feel the more embarrassed by reason of the remark of a boy who accused me of having forgotten to comb my hair.

This was not true, but the cap I wore always matted my hair down over my brow, and then, when I lifted it off invariably disarranged it completely. Nevertheless I felt guilty—and hot. I do suppose my hair was artistically barbered that night—I rather guess Mother had used the shears—and I can believe that I looked the half-wild colt that I was; but there was no call for that youth to direct attention to my unavoidable shagginess.

I don't think the tree had many candles, and I don't remember that it glittered with golden apples. But it was loaded with presents, and the girls coming and going clothed in bright garments made me forget my own looks—I think they made me forget to remove my overcoat, which was a sodden thing of poor cut and worse quality. I think I must have stood agape for nearly two hours listening: the songs, noting every motion of Adoniram Burtch and Asa Walker as they directed the ceremonies and prepared the way for the great event—that is to say, for the coming of Santa Claus himself.

A furious jingling of bells, a loud voice outside, the lifting of a window, the nearer clash of bells, and the dear old Saint appeared (in the person of Stephen Bartle) clothed in a red robe, a belt of sleigh bells, and a long white beard. The children cried out, "Oh!" The girls tittered and shrieked with excitement, and the boys laughed and clapped their hands. Then "Sandy" made a little speech about being glad to see us all, but as he had many other places to visit and as there were a great many presents to distribute, he guessed he'd have to ask some of the many pretty girls to help him. So he called upon Betty Burtch and Hattie Knapp—and I for one admired his taste, for they were the most popular maids of the school.

They came up blushing, and a little bewildered by the blaze publicity thus blown upon them. But their native dignity asserted itself, and the distribution of the presents began. I have a notion now that the fruit upon the tree was mostly bags of popcorn and "corny copias" of candy, but as my brother and I stood there that night and saw everybody, even the rowdiest boy, getting something we felt aggrieved and rebellious. We forgot that we had come from afar—we only knew that we were being left out.

But suddenly, in the midst of our gloom, my brother's name was called, and a lovely girl with a gentle smile handed him a bag of popcorn. My heart glowed with gratitude. Somebody had thought of us; and when she came to me, saying sweetly, "Here's something for you," I had no words to thank her. This happened nearly forty years ago, but her smile, her outstretched hand, her sympathetic eyes are vividly before me as I write. She was sorry for the shock-headed boy who stood against the wall, and her pity made the little box of candy a casket of pearls. The fact that I swallowed the jewels on the road home does not take from the reality of my adoration.

At last I had to take my final glimpse of that wondrous tree, and I well remember the walk home. My brother and I traveled in wordless companionship. The moon was sinking toward the west, and the snow crust gleamed with a million fairy lamps. The sentinel watchdogs barked from lonely farmhouses, and the wolves answered from the ridges. Now and then sleighs passed us with lovers sitting two and two, and the bells on their horses had the remote music of romance to us whose boots drummed like clogs of wood upon the icy road.

Our house was dark as we approached and entered it, but how deliciously warm it seemed after the pitiless wind! I confess we made straight for the cupboard for a mince pie, a doughnut and a bowl of milk!

As I write this there stands in my library a thick-branched, beautifully tapering fir tree covered with the gold and purple apples of Hesperides, together with crystal ice points, green and red and yellow candles, clusters of gilded grapes, wreaths of metallic frost, and glittering angels swinging in ecstasy; but I doubt if my children will ever know the keen pleasure (that is almost pain) which came to my brother and to me in those Christmas days when an orange was not a breakfast fruit, but a casket of incense and of spice, a message from the sunlands of the South.

That was our compensation—we brought to our Christmastime a keen appetite and empty hands. And the lesson of it all is, if we are seeking a lesson, that it is better to give to those who want than to those for whom "we ought to do something because they did something for us last year."

Never Underestimate the Power of Good

M. Norvel Young

The wind-whipped fire was raging out of control, galloping across Los Angeles County, charring homes, lives, and businesses as it went. The beautiful Malibu campus of Pepperdine University was trapped in the middle of the engulfing smoke and flames, like a terrified camper encircled by howling wolves in the night.

Hundreds of people had already lost their homes to the fire, and the houses on Tiner Court, where we live, were being evacuated. My wife, Helen, and I had been watching the news reports on television in our room in the Holiday Inn Crown Plaza in Bangkok, Thailand, where we were staying. We were praying constantly that homes and lives would be spared.

About six o'clock that evening, we quietly dressed for dinner and went to the lobby to meet one of our Pepperdine alumni.

Kumar Harilela, our host at the hotel, met us with a reserved smile, sharing our concern.

"Before we go to dinner, I have someone I'd like you to meet," he said. "This guest has been in the hotel for a week or so, resting."

We agreed and followed Kumar into the elevator. We arrived on the top floor and walked down the hall past the presidential suite, where Kumar had insisted we stay, to one of the single rooms at the end. He knocked quietly on the door and stepped back.

The door opened, and there stood . . . Mother Teresa!

The door opened, and there stood . . . Mother Teresa! I was surprised; I was thrilled; I was humbled. She smiled warmly and invited us in. We spent a precious half hour with Mother Teresa hearing about her work and answering her questions about ours. One comment she made stuck with me especially. She said, "I'm just so thankful to be able to help the poor."

She asked about Pepperdine and said she had been watching the fire and praying for those in danger. Then she took my right hand and said, "You remember the words of Jesus, 'Inasmuch as you do it unto the least of these my brethren . . .'" She paused, then completed Jesus's statement as she pointed to each of my five fingers in turn, "You do it unto me." I'll never forget the inspirational example of her life of service or her five-finger sermon. To do good to the lowliest is to serve the Lord Christ.

We came away from that small room amazed at her humility and quiet confidence. As we walked down the hall, back toward the elevator, I asked Kumar, "Why didn't you put *her* in the presidential suite?"

"I tried to, but she didn't feel that she deserved it."

The Thing about Goldfish

Marsha Arons

There are many good things about having a goldfish for a pet. It teaches even a small child a little responsibility. You don't have to walk it. It won't mess up the house. It doesn't shed. And one goldfish looks pretty much like another. This last trait is very important, I found, in light of the one bad thing about goldfish—they have a relatively short life span.

There are twelve years and two sisters between my oldest daughter, Anna, and my youngest, Elliana. But the two of them have always been close. So I wasn't surprised when it was Anna who solved the problem created by Elli's fear of the dark. We have four bedrooms in our house. When Elli graduated to a bed at age two and a half, we moved her in with her next oldest sister, Kayla. That left the two oldest girls with their own rooms, much to their delight. But Elli was afraid of the dark and Kayla couldn't sleep with a light on. Anna knew she would have to come up with something if she wanted to keep her personal space.

The answer was a goldfish. Anna bought Elli a bowl, a little plastic house for the fish to swim through, some colored gravel, and a small light that kept the little aquarium illuminated. Elli kept the bowl on the nightstand next to her bed. That way, she had enough light to make her feel safe and a "friend" to murmur to quietly

All of us became co-conspirators in the game of making sure that Elli always had a live goldfish in that bowl.

before she fell asleep. The light from the fish bowl was dim enough so that Kayla wasn't bothered. And both of them liked having a pet.

Elli fed that fish like clock-work and reminded us to clean the bowl more often than we would have liked. She was always careful about adding the anti-chlorine drops to the fresh water, lest her fish die a toxic death. And she named her fish creatively. Some days, the fish would be "Jaws"; other days, it would be "Swimmy." A few times, Elli decided its name was "Patsy" or "Mabel" or some other name that struck her fancy at a particular moment. The fish's gender also varied according to my daughter's whim.

But goldfish don't live very long. As a result, all of us became co-conspirators in the game of making sure that Elli always had a live goldfish in that bowl. Every night when I kissed her goodnight, I would check the fish. If I covered up my sleeping children in the middle of the night, I would check the fish. I found that Anna checked the fish, too, many times before she went to bed herself. If any of us noticed the fish looking a bit peaked around the gills, a quiet trip to the pet store was quickly scheduled. For fifty cents, we kept a little girl very happy. It was a small price to pay, to be sure, and Elli certainly never questioned her fish's longevity.

Elli turned six years old two weeks before Anna left for college. I was having a separation problem of my own sending my oldest off. But I was more worried about how Elli would react. In fact, Elli became quiet and spent a lot of time in her room for the first days after Anna left. But assured that she could send her sister pictures and talk to her on the phone, Elli, like the rest of us, adjusted. Still, it did feel odd to have five of us around the dinner table where there had once been six. But Anna was happy at school, and her enjoyment of her new surroundings made the transition easier for all of us.

One evening, as I was putting the two little ones to bed, Elli said to me, "Mommy, when this fish dies, will Anna come home and get me a new one?"

I don't know why I was surprised. Children don't really miss much, I guess. But I smiled at her and asked her how long she had known that her goldfish kept getting replaced every time one died. Elli just shrugged. I asked her if it bothered her that the present goldfish wasn't the same one her sister had bought for her almost four years before. No, it didn't bother her, Elli said. It never had. It had made Anna happy to play the game that way, so she just went along with it.

And so I understood. The little love token from one sister to another and back again was swimming happily beside my daughter's bed. The fish may not have been the original, but the message had never changed.

As I turned out the overhead light and watched the little aquarium glow softly, I thought, *Now I know one more good thing about goldfish!*

FRIENDS FOREVER

Jim McGuiggan

The girls obviously didn't think much of me when I was a teenager, so when this pretty girl called Ethel gave me more than a second look, I followed her like a lap dog and managed not to drive her away. Early in our relationship, we were walking down by the shoreline one evening, buttoned-up sweaters and scarves against the crisp air, arms around each other, her head in my chest, and she said to me, slowly but with some conviction, "Jim, I'm stuck on you." Forever unsure of myself, but with a nice warm flush rising in my face and wanting to hear more, I said, "Aw, you're probably just saying that." She said, "I'm not; my hair's caught in one of your buttons." You don't believe it, huh? Well . . . it's the kind of thing she might have said, for Ethel has a soft directness with her that I envy at times.

I could easily give you the impression that our relationship

227

over forty-three years of marriage has been ideal—that's just not so; but it's been a great adventure for all that. It's a marriage that's blossomed into friendship or maybe friendship that's blossomed into marriage. Perhaps something of both.

I've made more than my share of mistakes over the years and have many things to regret—things I can hardly bear to think about, much less reflect on—but there are some incidents that make me smile with pleasure and contentment, memories I bring out and examine more than occasionally.

We'll know each other, we'll still be us, and we'll be friends forever.

There was the time we were going through the Scriptures together and came across that enigmatic passage in Matthew 22:30 when Jesus's opponents asked him whose wife an often-married woman would be at the resurrection. Christ told them that husband-wife relationships wouldn't exist then. I said to Ethel, "That means you and I won't be husband and wife in that new phase of our existence." She struggled with that for a moment, not happy with it at all, but saying nothing. Seeing she was crestfallen and wanting to cheer her up, I quickly added, "But we'll know each other, we'll still be *us*, and we'll be friends forever."

That changed things totally, but it still moved her close to tears. She put her little hands over her eyes to hide them, and then, from between her fingers, her eyes glistening with tears, she looked out at me and said, "Is that really true, Jim?" By now I was all tenderness, moved by her pleasure and pleased at her joy, and I gently assured her it was. Friends forever.

THERE'S SOMETHING SO SPECIAL ABOUT THE GOLDEN OLDIES

Lynn M. Lombard

When I hear an Elvis Presley song or another "oldie but goodie," I am immediately swept back to my childhood. As I find myself singing in sync with the King, I'm thinking of someone entirely different. My dad. During family outings, car rides, and dinners, Dad always played music. I swear I must have heard those oldies while I was still in the womb.

When I first met my husband, he was amazed when I sang along with an oldies tune. "You know the words to this song?" he would question.

"Of course," I'd answer. "I grew up on this stuff."

I can picture Dad's expression while he's singing, his body swaying, not once missing a beat. When I go for my weekly visit to Mom and Dad's, their home is never silent. If the TV isn't on, the music is blaring with songs like "Earth Angel" or "Do Wah Diddy Diddy." He is my music lifeline because if there's anything he knows well, it's music. Ask him who sang a particular song from the 1950s or '60s, and he'll rattle off the answer from the archives of his jukebox memory.

Although today's teenagers would certainly question what an 8-track is, up until recently, Dad still had his entire collection tucked safely away. Then Mom, after years of trying, finally persuaded him to donate them. His 45 records, though, are a different matter. I imagine he'll never part with those. "They might be worth a lot of money someday," he says as an excuse. But I suspect money has nothing to do with it.

Along with those 45 records, albums, cassette tapes, and now compact discs compile his virtual mountain of music. His collection grows with each technological advance. Although he claims to hate spending money updating his stereo equipment, I know he secretly treasures every purchase.

While the family is playing a game of cards or enjoying a summer picnic, we never hear the same song. Dad's 200-CD player mixes a variety of his favorite tunes. It's amazing to see his transformation as he sets the mood of the night. Dad is my living proof that music soothes the body and relaxes the mind as I see the tension of his workday drift away.

I enjoy every moment of watching him. Every wedding reception I've attended with him (including mine), he seems to enjoy himself the most when he's out on the dance floor strutting his stuff. At home, whether he's by himself moving his body to the beat of the music or he's soothing his crying grandchildren by dancing with them until their tears evaporate, I am in my glory seeing my dad so happy.

Suddenly, tears roll down my face as I picture him one day soon holding my child in his arms, dancing as I know he once did with me. Maybe that's why I love the oldies. It has nothing to do with the music or the lyrics, but everything to do with the man who introduced them to me.

It has nothing to do with the music or the lyrics, but everything to do with the man who introduced them to me.

Dad said "my" music didn't compare. "His" music would always be better. "At least the songs I listen to tell a story," he would always say. As a teenager, I would argue the point, but today, as he's standing in my living room perusing my CD collection for one to borrow, I can only smile. Owning music that he actually enjoys listening to is proof that I'm my father's daughter.

Times will surely change and with it, the music and lyrics of the day. But nothing will ever compare to the "golden oldies" or replace the bond they've given me with my father.

THROUGH A FATHER'S EYES

Lonni Collins Pratt

I saw the car just before it hit me. I seemed to float. Then darkness smashed my senses.

I came to in an ambulance. Opening my eyes, I could see only shreds of light through my bandaged, swollen eyelids. I didn't know it then, but small particles of gravel and dirt were embedded in my freckled sixteen-year-old face. As I tried to touch it, someone tenderly pressed my arm down and whispered, "Lie still."

A wailing siren trailed distantly somewhere, and I slipped into unconsciousness. My last thoughts were a desperate prayer: "Dear God, not my face, please . . ."

Like many teenage girls, I found much of my identity in my appearance. Adolescence revolved around my outside image. Being pretty meant I had lots of dates and a wide circle of friends.

My father doted on me. He had four sons, but only one daughter. I remember one Sunday in particular. As we got out of the car at church, my brothers—a scruffy threesome in corduroy and cowlicks—ran ahead. Mom stayed home with the sick baby.

I was gathering my small purse, church school papers, and Bible. Dad opened the door. I looked up at him, convinced in my seven-year-old heart that he was more handsome and smelled better than any daddy anywhere.

He extended his hand to me with a twinkle in his eye and said, "A hand, my lady?" Then he swept me up into his arms and told me how pretty I was. "No father has ever loved a little girl more than I love you," he said.

In my child's heart, which didn't really understand a father's love, I thought it was my pretty dress and face he loved.

A few weeks before the accident, I had won first place in a local pageant, making me the festival queen. Dad didn't say much. He just stood with his arm over my shoulders, beaming with pride. Once more, I was his pretty little girl, and I basked in the warmth of his love and acceptance.

About this time, I made a personal commitment to Christ. In the midst of student council, honor society, pageants, and parades, I was beginning a relationship with God.

In the hours immediately after my accident, I drifted in and out of consciousness. Whenever my mind cleared even slightly, I wondered about my face. I was bleeding internally and had a severe concussion, but it never occurred to me that my concern with appearance was disproportionate.

The next morning, although I couldn't open my eyes more than a slit, I asked the nurse for a mirror. "You just concern yourself with getting well, young lady," she said, not looking at my face as she took my blood pressure.

Her refusal to give me a mirror only fueled irrational determination. If she wouldn't give me a mirror, I reasoned, it must be worse than I imagined. My face felt tight and itchy. It burned sometimes and ached other times. I didn't touch it, though, because my doctor told me that might cause infection.

My parents also battled to keep mirrors away. As my body healed internally and strength returned, I became increasingly difficult.

At one point, for the fourth time in less than an hour, I pleaded for a mirror. Five days had passed since the accident.

Angry and beaten down, Dad snapped, "Don't ask again! I said that's it!"

I wish I could offer an excuse for what I said. I propped myself on my elbows, and through lips that could barely move, hissed, "You don't love me. Now that I'm not pretty anymore, you just don't love me!"

Dad looked as if someone had knocked the life out of him. He slumped into a chair and put his head in his hands. My mother walked over and put her hand on his shoulder as he tried to control his tears. I collapsed against the pillows.

I didn't ask my parents for a mirror again. Instead, I waited until someone from housekeeping was straightening my room the next morning.

My curtain was drawn as if I were taking a sponge bath. "Could you get me a mirror, please?" I asked. "I must have mislaid mine." After a little searching, she found one and discreetly handed it to me around the curtain.

Nothing could have prepared me for what I saw. An image that resembled a giant scraped knee, oozing and bright pink, looked out at me. My eyes and lips were crusted and swollen. Hardly a patch of skin, ear-to-ear, had escaped the trauma.

My father arrived a little later with magazines and homework tucked under his arm. He found me staring into the mirror. Prying my fingers one by one from the mirror, he said, "It isn't important. This doesn't change anything that matters. No one will love you less."

Finally he pulled the mirror away and tossed it into a chair. He sat on the edge of my bed, took me in his arms, and held me for a long time.

"I know what you think," he said.

"You couldn't," I mumbled, turning away and staring out the window.

"You're wrong," he said, ignoring my self-pity.

"This will not change anything," he repeated. He put his hand on my arm, running it over an IV line. "The people who love you have seen you at your worst, you know."

"Right, seen me with rollers or with cold cream—not with my face ripped off!"

"Let's talk about me then," he said. "I love you. Nothing will ever change that because it's you I love, not your outside. I've changed your diapers and watched your skin blister with chicken pox. I've wiped up your bloody noses and held your head while you threw up in the toilet. I've loved you when you weren't pretty."

> *I love you. Nothing will ever change that because it's you I love, not your outside.*

He hesitated. "Yesterday you were ugly—not because of your skin, but because you behaved ugly. But I'm here today, and I'll be here tomorrow. Fathers don't stop loving their children, no matter what life takes. You will be blessed if life only takes your face."

I turned to my father, feeling it was all words, the right words, spoken out of duty—polite lies.

"Look at me then, Daddy," I said. "Look at me and tell me you love me."

I will never forget what happened next. As he looked into my battered face, his eyes filled with tears. Slowly, he leaned toward me, and with his eyes open, he gently kissed my scabbed, oozing lips.

It was the kiss that tucked me in every night of my young life, the kiss that warmed each morning.

Many years have passed. All that remains of my accident is a tiny indentation just above one eyebrow. But my father's kiss, and what it taught me about love, will never leave my lips.

SOURCE NOTES

CHAPTER ONE: *Hugs Are Gifts from the Heart*

"Middle Man" is excerpted from *Normal Is Just a Setting on Your Dryer* by Patsy Clairmont, a Focus on the Family book published by Tyndale House Publishers. Copyright © 1993, Patsy Clairmont. All rights reserved. International copyright secured. Used by permission. Patsy Clairmont is the author of numerous books including *God Uses Cracked Pots* and *I Grew Up Little*. Her newest release is *All Cracked Up*. Patsy is also a speaker for the Women of Faith conferences where she has spoken to over two million women in the past ten years.

"Stitches in Time" by Philip Gulley from *Hometown Tales* (Sisters, Ore.: Multnomah, 1998). Used by permission. Philip Gulley is a Quaker pastor, writer, and speaker. He lives in Indiana with his wife and two sons, Spencer and Sam.

"That's What Friends Do" by T. Suzanne Eller. Used by permission. Suzanne Eller is an author and speaker. She can be reached at tseller@daretobelieve.org.

"You Did This for Me?" by Max Lucado from *He Chose the Nails* (Nashville: W Publishing, a division of Thomas Nelson, Inc., 2000). Reprinted by permission. All rights reserved.

"Unexpected Gifts" by Nance Guilmartin from *Healing Conversations: What to Say When You Don't Know What to Say* (Hoboken, N.J.: John Wiley, 2002). Reprinted with permission of John Wiley & Sons, Inc.

SOURCE NOTES

"Little Chad" by Dale Galloway from *Rebuild Your Life* (Wheaton, Ill.: Tyndale, 1980). Used by permission.

CHAPTER TWO: *Hugs Teach Lessons from the Heart*

"Personal Testimony" by Nika Maples. Used by permission.

"An Awesome Deal" by Katherine Grace Bond. Used by permission. Katherine Grace Bond is the author of the bestselling *Legend of the Valentine*. Visit her at www.katherinegracebond.com.

"Power of the Powerless: A Brother's Lesson" by Christopher de Vinck. Reprinted from the *Wall Street Journal* © 1985 Dow Jones & Company. All rights reserved. Used by permission. Christopher de Vinck, author of eleven books, lives with his wife, Roe, in Pompton Plains, New Jersey.

"Dance of the Blue Butterfly" by Cathy Lee Phillips from *Gutsy Little Flowers* (Canton, Ga.: Patchwork Press, 2001). Used by permission. www.cathyleephillips.com.

"The Stranger with a Life in His Luggage" by Dianna Booher from *Well Connected* (Nashville: W Publishing, a division of Thomas Nelson, Inc., 2000). All rights reserved.

"Perfect Gift" by Shelley F. Mickle from *The Kids Are Gone, The Dog Is Depressed, and Mom's on the Loose* (Gainesville, Fla.: Alachua Press, 2000).

CHAPTER THREE: *Hugs Show Love from the Heart*

"Dwelling in Grace" by Britta Coleman. Used by permission. Britta Coleman (www.brittacoleman.com) is an award-winning author, journalist, and inspirational speaker. Her debut novel, *Potter Springs*, won the Lone Star Scribe Award, and her "Practically Parenting" column is published as a regular newspaper feature. Britta lives in Fort Worth, Texas, with her husband, two children, and two Chihuahuas.

"The Prince's Happy Heart," a folktale.

"My Son, the Teacher" by Zig Ziglar from *Confessions of a Happy Christian* (Gretna, La.: Pelican Publishing, Inc., 1978). Used by permission of the publisher.

SOURCE NOTES

"The Birthday Balloon" by Sharla Taylor. Used by permission. Sharla Taylor is a freelance writer who lives in Richmond Hill, Georgia with her husband, youngest son, and yellow Lab puppy. She also has two absolutely terrific adult children who are completing their college educations. Sharla's business Web site is www.athomewithwords.com, and her author's Web site is www.sharlataylor.com.

"Mother's Day Breakfast" by Patti Maguire Armstrong from *Amazing Grace for Mothers* (West Chester, Pa.: Ascension Press, 2004). Used by permission.

"Love's Power" taken from *The Friendship Factor* by Alan Loy McGinnis, copyright ©1979 Augsburg Publishing House. Used by permission of Augsburg Fortress.

CHAPTER FOUR: *Hugs Whisper Prayers to the Heart*

"Before You Ask" by Helen Roseveare. Used by permission.

"The Owl and the Pelican" by Billy Graham from *Unto the Hills* (Nashville: W Publishing, a division of Thomas Nelson, Inc., 1996). Reprinted by permission. All rights reserved.

"T and D" by Vicki P. Graham. Used by permission of the author.

"Junior" by Amy Hollingsworth from *The Simple Faith of Mr. Rogers* (Nashville: Integrity, 2005). Used by permission.

"The Faith of a Child" by Jennifer Mihills, copyright © 2006. Used by permission of the author.

"Minor—Traveling Unattended" by Jerry Seiden from *Michael's Stable* (Irvine, Calif.: Spirit of Hope, 1999). www.spiritofhopepublishing.com.

CHAPTER FIVE: *Hugs Bring Hope to the Heart*

"Memories and Promises by the Crab Apple Tree" by Cathy Lee Phillips from *Gutsy Little Flowers* (Canton, Ga.: Patchwork Press, 2001). Used by permission. www.cathyleephillips.com.

"The Teacher's Challenge" by India M. Allmon. Used by permission.

"Remember the Frandsens" by Kathryn Forbes from *The World's Best Bathroom Book* (Colorado Springs: Honor Books, 2005). Used by permission. To order, www.cookministries.com. All rights reserved.

SOURCE NOTES

"Twice Blessed" by Nancy Jo Eckerson, copyright © 1999. Used by permission. For more information on this or any other stories by author please contact folknanc@yahoo.com.

"Party in Room 210" by Tony Campolo from *Let Me Tell You A Story* (Nashville: W Publishing, a division of Thomas Nelson, Inc., 2000). Reprinted by permission. All rights reserved.

"A Little Glimpse of Heaven" by Chuck Terrill from *Hope and Hilarity* (Kearney, Neb.: Morris Publishing, 1996). Used by permission of the author, chuck@vcchristianchurch.com. For more articles by author, visit www .arkvalleynews.com.

CHAPTER SIX: *Hugs Make Music in the Heart*

"The Gift of Caring" by Arthur Gordon from *A Touch of Wonder* (Grand Rapids: Fleming H. Revell, a division of Baker Publishing Group, 1974).

"Music Lessons" by Katherine Grace Bond. Used by permission. Katherine Grace Bond is the author of the bestselling *Legend of the Valentine*. Visit her at www.katherinegracebond.com.

"The Invitation" by Mary Hollingsworth. Administered by Shady Oaks Studio, 1507 Shirley Way, Bedford, TX 76022. All rights reserved. Used by permission.

"Beautiful Dreamer" by Arthur Gordon from *A Touch of Wonder* (Grand Rapids: Fleming H. Revell, a division of Baker Publishing Group, 1974).

"Recapture the Wonder" by Ravi Zacharias from *Recapture the Wonder* (Nashville: Integrity Publishers, 2003). Used by permission.

"The Duet" by Charlotte Greeson. Administered by Shady Oaks Stuio, 1507 Shirley Way, Bedford, TX 76022. All rights reserved. Used by permission of author.

CHAPTER SEVEN: *Hugs Create Joy in the Heart*

"A Box of Broken Dreams" by Florence Littauer from *I've Found My Keys, Now Where's My Car?* Used by permission of author. Florence Littauer is founder of The CLASSeminar, speaker, and author of *Silver Boxes* and *Personality Plus.* http://www.classervices.com.

"Let's Go Bug Hunting" by Barbara Russell Chesser. Used by permission of author.

"A Story for Valentine's Day" by Jo Ann Larsen.

"Dinner-Plate Dahlias" by Melodie M. Davis from *Why Didn't I Just Raise Radishes?* (Scottdale, Pa.: Mennonite Publishing Network, 1994). Used by permission.

"A Little Good News" by M. Norvel Young from *Living Lights, Shining Stars* (West Monroe, La.: Howard Books, 1997).

"The Wrong One" by Tony Campolo from *Let Me Tell You a Story* (Nashville: W Publishing, a division of Thomas Nelson, Inc., 2000). Reprinted by permission. All rights reserved.

CHAPTER EIGHT: *Hugs Are Touches of the Heart*

"My First Christmas Tree" by Hamlin Garland. First appeared in *Ladies Home Journal,* Vol. 28, December, 1911.

"Never Underestimate the Power of Good" by M. Norvel Young from *Living Lights, Shining Stars* (West Monroe, La.: Howard Books, 1997).

"The Thing about Goldfish" by Marsha Arons. Used by permission of author.

"Friends Forever" by Jim McGuiggan from *Let Me Count the Ways* (West Monroe, La:. Howard Books, 2001).

"There's Something So Special about the Golden Oldies" by Lynn M. Lombard. Used by permission of author.

"Through a Father's Eyes" by Lonni Collins Pratt, copyright © 1992. Used by permission.